Macs
FOR
DUMMIES®
PORTABLE EDITION

by Edward C. Baig

WILEY

Wiley Publishing, Inc.

Macs For Dummies®, Portable Edition

Published by
Wiley Publishing, Inc.
111 River Street
Hoboken, NJ 07030-5774

www.wiley.com

Copyright © 2010 by Wiley Publishing, Inc., Indianapolis, Indiana

Published by Wiley Publishing, Inc., Indianapolis, Indiana

Published simultaneously in Canada

For general information on our other products and services, please contact our Customer Care Department within the U.S. at 877-762-2974, outside the U.S. at 317-572-3993, or fax 317-572-4002.

For technical support, please visit www.wiley.com/techsupport.

Wiley also publishes its books in a variety of electronic formats. Some content that appears in print may not be available in electronic books.

ISBN: 978-0-470-59141-3

Manufactured in the United States of America

10 9 8 7 6 5 4 3 2 1

WILEY

Table of Contents

Chapter 7: Handling Trouble 121

Chapter 8: Ten Clever Dashboard Widgets. 131

Introduction

● ●

*W*hat an amazing time to get to know the Mac. For years these elegantly designed computers have been a model of simplicity and virus-free stability. But that's never stopped Apple from making these machines even harder to resist by applying stunning changes.

Consider Apple's seismic embrace of Intel a few years ago. It means you, Mr. or Ms. Computer Buyer, can have your cake and eat it too. (I love a good cliché when I need it.) You can benefit from what remains the best marriage in personal computing (the blessed union between Mac hardware and Mac software), but you no longer have to ditch the Microsoft Windows–based software you currently use out of habit, due to business obligations, or because you don't know any better.

About This Book

A word about the *For Dummies* franchise I'm proud to be a part of: These books are built around the idea that all of us feel like dopes whenever we tackle something new, especially when the subject at hand (technology) reeks of a jargon-y stench.

I happen to know you don't have a dummy bone in your body, and the publishers at Wiley know it too. Au contraire. (How dumb can you be if you speak French?) If anything, you've already demonstrated smarts by purchasing this book. You're ready to plunge into the best computing environment I know of.

I'm a relative latecomer to the Mac. I grew up on MS-DOS computing and then migrated like most of the rest of the world to Windows. I still use Windows machines every day. But I've since become a devoted Mac convert and I use my various Apples every day too. (No snide remarks, please; I find time for other pursuits.)

When writing this book, I vowed to keep the geek-speak to a minimum. I couldn't eliminate it entirely, and to be honest, I wouldn't want to. Here's why:

- ✔ You may come across absurdly complicated terms in advertisements and on the Web, so it's helpful to have at least a passing familiarity with some of them.

- ✔ Nothing says we can't poke a little fun now and then at the nerds who drummed up this stuff.

Conventions Used in This Book

Anyone who has skimmed the pages of this or other *For Dummies* books knows they're not exactly *War and Peace.* Come to think of it, it's too bad Tolstoy got to that name first. It would make a great title when the definitive account of the Apple-Intel alliance is written.

Macs For Dummies, Portable Edition, makes generous use of numbered and bulleted lists and screen grabs captured, by the way, using a handy little freebie Mac utility (invaluable to writers of books like this) called Grab. See, you haven't even escaped the introduction, and I threw in your first Mac lesson, just like that.

How This Book Is Organized

Chapter 1 provides an overview of the Mac and its
iLife software. Chapter 2 is a brief tour of Mac-specific
settings, keyboard keys, and its ports and connectors.

In Chapter 3, you are introduced to the Mac desktop,
including the dock, Stacks, the Mac window and its
different window views, and the Quick Look feature.
You even find out about some free programs.

Chapter 4 lets you know everything you can do to
truly make your Mac your own, from establishing
your account to making personal settings. With as
much fun as you'll have with your Mac, eventually
you'll have to use it to get some work done, and that
is what Chapter 5 is all about.

In Chapter 6 you really move into the fun stuff, from
setting up e-mail and browsing with Safari to manag-
ing your music and importing, retouching, and sharing pictures. Need to solve a problem? Head straight
to Chapter 7 and do not pass Go. The book concludes
with Chapter 8, which tells you about ten great dashboard widgets.

Icons Used in This Book

Sprinkled in the margins of these pages are round
little pictures, or icons. I could have easily mentioned
icons in the "Conventions Used in This Book" section,
because icons are *For Dummies* conventions too, not
to mention essential ingredients in today's computers. I use three of them throughout this book.

 I present the Tip icon when a shortcut or recom-
mendation might make the task at hand faster
or simpler.

A Remember icon means a point of emphasis is here. So along with remembering your spouse's birthday and where you put the house keys, you might want to retain some of this stuff.

The Warning icon is my way of saying pay heed to this passage and proceed gingerly, lest you wreak the kind of havoc that can cause real and possibly permanent damage to your computer and (by extension) your wallet.

Where to Go from Here

The beauty of the *For Dummies* format is that you can jump around and read any section you want. You're not obliged to follow a linear structure. Need to find out where to plug something in? Head straight to Chapter 2 and do not pass Go. Want to e-mail photos to a friend? Meet me in Chapter 6. You bring the coffee.

Above all, I hope you have fun reading the book, and more importantly, I hope you have a grand old time with your Mac. Thanks for buying the book.

Chapter 1

Adventuring into the Mac World

● ●

In This Chapter

▶ Discovering why your computer is special

▶ Conversing with your computer

▶ Introducing iLife

● ●

*F*orgive me for getting too personal right off the bat, but next to your spouse or significant other, is there anyone or anything you touch more often than a computer keyboard? Or gaze at more intensely than a monitor?

If this is your initial dalliance with a Macintosh, you are probably already smitten — and quite possibly at the start of a lifelong affair.

Despite its good looks, the Mac is much more than a trophy computer. You can admire the machine for flaunting intelligent design, versatility, and toughness. A Mac can take care of itself. As of this writing, the Mac has avoided the scourge of viruses that plague PCs based on Microsoft Windows. Apple's darlings are a lot more stable too, so they crash and burn less often.

Mac-Spectacular Computing

You shouldn't be alarmed that far fewer people own Macs compared with PCs. That's like saying fewer people drive Ferraris than drive Chevys. Strength in numbers is overrated.

Besides, as a new member of the Mac community, consider the company you are about to keep. Mac owners tend to belong to the cool crowd: artists, designers, performers, and (can't resist this one) writers.

Sure, these same people can be smug at times. I've had Mac mavens go ballistic on me for penning *positive* reviews that were not flattering enough. Or for even daring to suggest that Macs aren't always perfect.

The machines come pretty darn close, though, so if you're new to the Mac you're in for a treat. It has been suggested that most Windows users go to their computers to complete the task at hand and be done with it. The Mac owner also gets things done, of course. The difference is that machines branded with the Apple logo tend to be a labor of love. Moreover, now that Intel is inside newer Macs, Apple's computer can double as a pretty darn effective Windows machine.

Oh, and you'll always remember the first time.

Checking out shapes and sizes

When people speak of the Mac, they may refer to both the physical machine (or hardware) and the *operating system* software that makes it all tick. One is worthless without the other. On a Mac, the operating system is called *OS X* (pronounced "oh-S-ten"). The seventh major release of OS X also carries a ferocious moniker, Snow Leopard.

Apple Computer has a tremendous advantage over the companies promoting Windows PCs because it's the single entity responsible for producing not only the computer itself but also the important software that choreographs the way the system behaves. Everything is simpatico.

That's in stark contrast to the ways of the PC world. Companies such as Dell and Hewlett-Packard manufacture hardware. Microsoft produces the Windows software that fuels the machines. Sure these companies maintain close ties, but they just don't share Apple's blood relationships.

You'll find a variety of Macintoshes meant to sit on top of your desk, thus the term *desktop computer.* Just know for now that the main examples of the breed are the iMac, the Mac mini, and the Mac Pro.

Mac *laptops,* so named because they rest on your lap and are portable, include the MacBook, the MacBook Pro, and the twiggy-thin MacBook Air. They're sometimes referred to as *notebook computers* or just plain *notebooks.* As with spiral notebooks, they can fit into a briefcase.

Matching a Mac to your needs

Haven't settled on which Mac to buy? This book provides assistance. Cheap advice: If you can eyeball the computers in person, by all means do so. Apple operates more than 200 retail stores worldwide, mostly in North America. Trolling through these high-tech candy stores is a delight. Of course, you can also buy Macs on the Internet or in traditional "brick and mortar" computer stores.

Just be prepared to part with some loot. Although the gap between the cost of PCs and Macs is narrowing, you'll typically pay more for a Mac versus a comparable unit on the PC side.

(Uh oh! The Mac diehards are boiling at that remark: I can practically see their heads exploding as they rant: "There is no such thing as a *comparable* Windows machine.")

 Keep in mind that students are often eligible for discounts on computers. Check with your college or university bookstore. Apple also gives breaks to faculty, administrators, and K-12 teachers.

You might also qualify for a corporate discount through your employer.

Selecting handy peripherals

As you might imagine, a full range of peripherals complement the Mac. Although much of what you create in *bits* and *bytes,* to put it in computer-speak, stays in that electronic form, at some point you're probably going to want to print your work. On old-fashioned paper, no less. Fortunately, a number of excellent printers work with Macs.

You may also choose a *scanner,* which in some respects is the opposite of a printer. That's because you start with an image already in paper form, and scan, or translate, it into a form your computer can understand and display. Okay, so you can also scan from slides or microfiche but you get my point.

Some machines combine printing and scanning functions, often with copier and fax capabilities as well. These are called *multifunction,* or all-in-one, devices.

Communicating with Your Mac

The Mac isn't at all standoffish like some human objects of affection. It's friendly and approachable. In this section, I tell you how.

It's a GUI

Every mainstream computer in operation today employs what's called a _graphical user interface,_ or GUI. The Mac's GUI is arguably the most inviting of all. It consists of colorful objects or pictures on your screen, plus windows and menus (for more, see Chapter 3). You interact with these using a computer _mouse_ or other _pointing device_ to tell your machine and its various programs how to behave. Sure beats typing instructions as arcane commands or taking a crash course in programming.

Even though GUI is pronounced "gooey," there's nothing remotely yucky about it.

With great tools for you

Given its versatility, I've often thought a Mac would make a terrific product to peddle on one of those late-night infomercials. _"It slices, it dices. Why it even does more than a Ginsu Knife or Popeil Pocket Fisherman!"_

Indeed, have you ever paused to consider what a computer is anyhow? Let's consider a few of its most primitive (albeit handy) functions. A Mac can

- Tell time
- Display family portraits
- Solve arithmetic problems
- Play movies
- Let you chat with friends

I dare say you didn't surrender a grand or two for a simple clock, photo album, calculator, DVD player, or telephone. But it's sure nice having all those capabilities in one place, and as that announcer on TV might bark, _"That's not all folks."_

I can't possibly rattle off all the nifty things a Mac can do in one section (besides, I encourage you to read the rest of the book). But whether you bought or intend to buy a Mac for work, play, or more likely some combination of the two, some little birdie tells me the contents of the Mac's tool chest will surpass your expectations.

And output, too

I'm confident that you'll spend many pleasurable hours in front of your computer. At the end of the day, though, you're going to want to show other people how productive and clever you've been. So whether you produce legal briefs, spiffy newsletters for the PTA, or music CDs for your fraternity's big bash, the Mac will make you proud.

Living the iLife

All the latest Macs are loaded with a terrific suite of software programs called iLife to help you master the digital lifestyle you are about to become accustomed to. (On older systems, you can purchase the upgraded iLife suite of programs.) I dig deeper into the iTunes and iPhoto components of iLife in Chapter 6. Here's a sneak preview of what iLife has to offer:

- ✓ **iPhoto:** The great photographer Ansel Adams would have had a field day with iPhoto. This software lets you organize and share your best pictures in myriad ways, including placing them in calendars or in coffee table books.

- ✓ **iMovie:** Can an Academy Award be far behind? iMovie is all about applying cinematic effects to turn your video into a piece of high-minded art that would make Martin Scorsese proud. Who knows, maybe Apple boss Steve Jobs will find work for you at Disney or Pixar.

✔ **iDVD:** Use this program to create DVDs with chapters, like the films you rent at the video store.

✔ **GarageBand:** Did somebody mention groupies? GarageBand lets you make music using virtual software instruments. The latest version also helps you create online radio shows, or *podcasts.*

✔ **iWeb:** This member of the iLife troupe is all about helping you create your own Web site.

Chapter 2

The Nuts and Bolts
of Your Mac

- -

In This Chapter

▶ Turning on the computer and getting set up

▶ Taming the mouse

▶ Keying in on the keyboard

▶ Finding common ports and connectors

- -

*H*ave you taken the plunge and purchased the computer? If so, you've made a fabulous decision.

I bet you're dying to get started. You might even have begun without reading these initial instructions. Fine with me. No offense taken. The Mac is intuitive, after all, and the title on this cover notwithstanding, you're no dummy. I know because you had the good sense to buy a Macintosh — and this book. Besides, what would it say about Apple's product designers if they couldn't make you understand how to turn on the computer?

If you didn't jump the gun, that's cool too. That's why your humble servant, um, author, is here.

Turning On and Tuning In Your Mac

To borrow a line from a famous musical, "Let's start at the very beginning, a very good place to start . . ." In the *Do-Re-Mi*'s of Macintosh computing, plugging the computer in the wall is a very good place to start. It doesn't get a whole lot more complicated from there.

The On button

Take a second to locate the round On, or power, button. Where it resides depends on the Mac model you purchased, but finding it shouldn't be too taxing. I'll even give away the secret on recently-issued models. For the latest iMac, the On button is on the lower-left back panel of the monitor (when you are facing the monitor). For Mac laptops, the button is to the right of the keyboard.

Go ahead and press the On button now. Explosive things are about to happen. Not those kinds of explosives; it's just that igniting your first session on the Mac makes you *da bomb* (translation: college slang for awesome or cool).

To let you know that all is peachy (or should I say Apple-y), you hear a musical chime while the Apple logo briefly shows up on the screen in front of a gray background.

Creating an identity

You're almost ready to begin touring the computer. But not quite. An important step remains. You must choose an identity, or *user account,* to tell the Mac that you are the Grand Poobah of this particular computer. As this almighty administrator, you and you alone can subsequently add accounts for other members of your family or workplace, each with a password that keeps them from snooping into one another's computing workspace.

Type the name of the account holder (for example, *Cookie Monster*), the short name (*Cookie*), the password (*chocolatechip* or better yet something that's harder to guess), and the password again to verify it. You are also asked to type a password hint (*yummy flavor*) as a gentle reminder should you ever forget your password. Failing to remember things might not happen to you, but it sure happens to me.

On models with a built-in camera you'll also be asked at this stage to choose an account picture. Better not be camera-shy, because this too you can't refuse.

Clocking in

Because it probably already seems like day is turning into night, this is as appropriate a time as any to, well, select your time zone by clicking near where you live on the world map that appears. If you're connected to the Internet, the computer already knows the date and time. If not, you can enter them now.

Registering your Mac

When all is said and done, the nice folks at Apple would also like you to register your Mac. You can put this off till later or skip it. Letting Apple know who you are gives the company the opportunity to flood you with promotional e-mail. But you can register and opt-out of promotional e-mail.

Shutting down

We began this section with a noble discussion of how to turn on the Mac. (Humor me if you didn't think the discussion was even remotely noble.) So even though you barely have your feet wet, I'm going to tell you how to turn the dang thing off. Don't you just hate people who not only give away the ending (it's the butler) but also tell you to do something and then tell you why you shouldn't have done it?

Okay. Ready? Sayonara time.

Using the arrow-shaped *cursor,* which you control with your mouse, stab the small logo found at the upper-left corner of the screen. Click once, and a drop-down menu appears. Move the cursor down until the Shut Down entry is highlighted. You know a command or an entry is highlighted because a blue strip appears over its name.

Pressing Enter on the keyboard or clicking Shut Down brings up what's called a *dialog box* (see Figure 2-1). I'm no shrink, but it's obvious based on the question the computer asks inside this box that it suffers from separation anxiety. "Are you *sure* you want to shut down your computer now?"

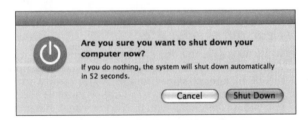

Are you sure you want to shut down your computer now?

If you do nothing, the system will shut down automatically in 52 seconds.

Cancel   Shut Down

Figure 2-1: Are you sure you want to shut down?

Do nothing, and the machine will indeed turn itself off in a minute on Snow Leopard machines or two minutes on older Macs. If you want to say "so long" immediately, click the button labeled Shut Down. If you hold down the Option key when choosing Shut Down, this dialog is bypassed.

Having second thoughts? Click Cancel.

Mousing Around the Interface

By now you're catching on to the idea that this computing business requires a lot more clicking than Dorothy had to do to get back to Kansas. She used ruby slippers. You get to use a mouse.

A computer mouse is generally less frightening than that other kind of critter. In keeping with this *Wizard of Oz* comparison, not even the Cowardly Lion would be scared of it. And though your high-tech rodent can get finicky at times, you're unlikely to set traps to bring about its demise.

Some mice connect to the computer through cords. Some mice are wireless. (And laptops use trackpads.) In each case, they're called *pointing devices* because — brace yourself for this advanced concept — they're devices that sort of point.

I'll explain. You roll the mouse across a flat surface (typically your desk, perhaps a specialized mouse pad). As you do so, a cursor, or insertion point, on the screen miraculously apes the movement of your hand gliding the mouse. (Note to self: The mixed metaphor police, a.k.a. my editor, must love the mention of a mouse and a monkey in the same breath.) If the mouse loses touch with the surface of your desk, the cursor will no longer move.

When you place the cursor precisely where you want it, you're ready for the clicking part. Place your index finger on the upper-left portion of the mouse, press down quickly, and let go. You'll hear a clicking sound, and in some cases your entire body will tingle with satisfaction. You have indeed mastered the fine art of clicking.

Don't get too cocky. Now try *double-clicking,* an action often required to get something accomplished. You're pretty much repeating the preceding exercise, only now you're clicking twice in rapid succession while keeping the cursor in the same location. It may take a little practice. But you'll get it.

Left- and right-clicking

If you've been using a Windows computer, you're accustomed to working with a mouse that has two or more buttons. More times than not you click, or double-click, using the upper-left button. That's where the remarkably unoriginal name of *left-clicking* comes from. Left-clicking usually serves the purpose of selecting things on the screen. By contrast, the opposite action, *right-clicking,* brings up a menu of shortcut commands.

Until recently, the typical Apple mouse had just one button, the functional equivalent of the left button on a Windows mouse. (Apple's programmable Mighty Mouse, included with recent Macs, can behave like a multibutton mouse.) Having just one button on a Mac is less of a big deal than you might think. That's because you can effectively right-click, or bring up a shortcut menu, with a one-button Mac mouse anyway. To accomplish this great feat, press Control on the keyboard while you click.

Pointing and clicking on a laptop

You can attach a regular mouse to any Mac laptop, but it is not always convenient to use one when you're on a 747 or working in tight quarters.

Fortunately, Mac portables have something called a *trackpad,* a smooth area just below the keyboard. You glide your finger on the trackpad to choreograph the movement of the cursor. The button just below the trackpad handles clicking chores.

What a drag

The mouse is responsible for at least one other important bit of business: *dragging.* Position the cursor on top of the symbol or icon you want to drag. Then hold down the mouse button and roll the mouse across your desk. As you do so, the icon moves to a new location on the screen.

Knowing What's Handy about the Keyboard

As with any computer — or an old-fashioned type-writer for that matter — the Mac keyboard is laid out in *QWERTY* style, meaning the top row of letters starts with *Q, W, E, R, T,* and *Y.* But a computer keyboard also contains a bunch of specialized keys that the inventors of the typewriter wouldn't have dreamed of.

Finding the major functions

The top row of the Mac keyboard carries a bunch of keys with the letter *F* followed by a number. From left to right, you go from F1, F2, F3, all the way out (in some cases) to F16. These are your loyal *function keys* (also called *F keys*), and their particular marching orders vary among Mac models. Depending on your setup, pressing certain F keys has no effect at all.

On Mac laptops, the F1 and F2 keys can raise or lower the brightness of your screen. On other types of Macs, F14 and F15 perform those functions. Again there are exceptions.

Those various F keys may be difficult to spot at first on a laptop. They have teeny-tiny labels and share keys. You'll have to press the fn key at the same time you press a function key to make it, well, function as a function key. Otherwise such keys will perform their other duties.

The keys you use every day

Quick quiz: Guess which keys you employ most often? Too easy. The keys you use every day are the ones representing vowels and letters with low point values in *Scrabble*.

Naturally, these aren't the only keys that work over-time. The spacebar, comma, and period are darn busy. If you're into hyperbole, the exclamation mark key puts in an honest day's effort too. Don't let me shortchange Shift or Return. And I know you accountants in the crowd spend a lot of time hammering away at all those number keys.

More keys to success

You'll find these other keys extremely useful:

- ✔ **esc:** The great Escape key. The equivalent of clicking Cancel in a dialog box.

✔ ◆ ◆)) ◆: These raise, lower, or mute the volume of the computer's speakers, though in laptops certain function keys perform these duties.

✔ ⏏: No doubt this is James Bond's favorite key. Press it, and one of two things is supposed to happen. On most newer Macs, a CD or DVD loaded inside the guts of the computer spits out of a hidden slot. On other models, the tray holding the disc slides out.

✔ **Delete, delete:** You aren't reading double. Some Mac keyboards have two delete keys, each with a different assignment. Regular delete is your backspace key. Press it, and it erases the character directly to the left of the cursor. The second delete key, which sometimes appears as Del and sometimes as delete accompanied by an x inside a small pentagon, is the forward delete key. It wipes out the character to the right of the cursor. Confusingly, on some laptops and with a new aluminum keyboard, you can purge the letter to the right of the cursor by pressing fn and delete at the same time.

✔ **Home, End:** The jumpiest keys you'll come across. Press Home and you're instantly vaulted to the top of the document or Web page window in which you are working. Press End and you often plunge to the bottom, depending on the application.

✔ **Page Up, Page Down:** A keyboard alternative for moving up or down one huge gulp or screenful at a time.

✔ **Option:** Pressing Option (labeled Alt Option on some keyboards) while you press another key generates symbols. You can't possibly recall them all, though over time, you'll learn the key combinations for symbols you regularly call upon. For example, press Option and 2 for ™,

Option and V for √, and Option and R for ®. Feel free to play around with other combinations.

✔ **Control:** The Control key and the mouse click make a powerful combination. Control-clicking yields pop-up *contextual menus* that only make sense in the moment. For example, Control-clicking a term in the Microsoft Word word processing program brings up a menu that lets you find a synonym for that word, among other options. Because finding a synonym doesn't make a lot of sense when you control-click a picture in iPhoto, the action opens up different possibilities, including editing, rotating, and duplicating an image.

✔ **⌘:** Pressing this cloverleaf key at the same time you press another keyboard character creates keyboard shortcuts, a subject worthy of its own topic (see the next section).

Taking a shortcut

If you hold the mouse in high regard, you may want to give the little fellow time off now and then. That's the beauty of keyboard shortcuts. When you simultaneously press ⌘ and a given key, stuff happens. You just have to remember which combination of keys to use under which circumstances.

To understand how such shortcuts work, consider the popular act of copying material from one program and reproducing it in another. You are about to practice *copy-and-paste* surgery.

I present two ways to do this. One leaves pretty much everything up to your mouse. The other, while still using the mouse a little, mainly exploits keyboard shortcuts.

The first option follows:

1. **Use the mouse to highlight, or select, the passage you want to copy.**

2. **On the menu bar at the top of the screen, choose Edit⇨Copy.**

3. **Move the mouse and click to place your mouse at the point where you want to paste the text.**

4. **Choose Edit⇨Paste.**

   The copied material magically appears at its new destination.

Here is the keyboard shortcut method:

1. **Highlight the text you want to copy.**

2. **Hold down the ⌘ key while you press the C key.**

   The result is the same as if you had clicked Edit and Copy.

3. **Move the mouse and click to place the mouse at the point where you want to paste.**

4. **Press ⌘ and the V key.**

   You just pasted the text.

Many clickable menu items have keyboard equivalents. These shortcuts are displayed in the various menus to the right of their associated commands, as shown in Figure 2-2. Note that some keyboard shortcuts shown in the menu appear dimmed. That's because the commands can't be used at this particular point. And some shortcuts require both the ⌘ key and one or more additional modifier keys, as in Shift+⌘+N for a New Folder.

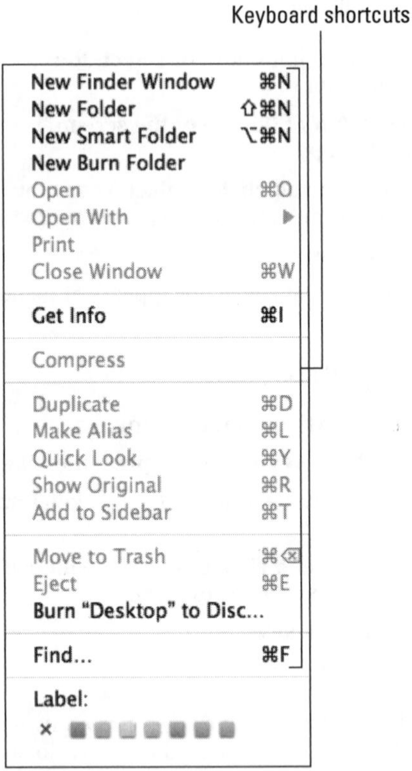

Keyboard shortcuts

New Finder Window	⌘N
New Folder	⇧⌘N
New Smart Folder	⌥⌘N
New Burn Folder	
Open	⌘O
Open With	▶
Print	
Close Window	⌘W
Get Info	⌘I
Compress	
Duplicate	⌘D
Make Alias	⌘L
Quick Look	⌘Y
Show Original	⌘R
Add to Sidebar	⌘T
Move to Trash	⌘⌫
Eject	⌘E
Burn "Desktop" to Disc...	
Find...	⌘F
Label:	
✕ ■ ■ ■ ■ ■ ■ ■	

Figure 2-2: To use a keyboard shortcut or not to? That is the question.

Locating the Common Ports and Connectors

Industry-standard jacks, holes, and connectors on the back or side of your Mac (depending on whether you have a desktop or laptop) may look funky. But you can't live without (most of) them. They are your bridge to the gaggle of devices and peripherals that want to have a relationship with your computer (see Figure 2-3).

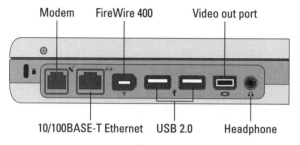

Modem   FireWire 400   Video out port

10/100BASE-T Ethernet   USB 2.0   Headphone

Figure 2-3: Hook me up, Scotty.

The *Universal Serial Bus,* or USB, connects printers, scanners, digital cameras, Webcams, iPods, joysticks, speakers, keychain disk drives, piano keyboards, and even your mouse and computer keyboard to your Mac.

FireWire is a speedy connector often used with digital camcorders. But it also connects iPods and external hard drives.

The end of the cable that plugs in to an *Ethernet* jack looks just like a phone jack on steroids. In fact, Ethernet and phone cords are easily mistaken. Ethernet's main purpose is to provide a fast outlet to the Internet or your office computer network.

Chapter 3

Getting to the Core of the Apple

● ●

In This Chapter

▶ Traveling around the desktop

▶ Introducing the menu bar

▶ Getting to know icons, folders, and windows

▶ Sneaking a Quick Look

▶ Demystifying the dock

▶ Stocking Stacks

▶ Discovering cool software

● ●

*A*lthough I'm quite positive he never used a personal computer a day in his life, the wise Chinese philosopher Confucius could have had the Mac in mind when he said, "If you enjoy what you do, you'll never work another day in your life." People surely enjoy their Macs, even when they *are* doing work on the machine. Before you can totally whoop it up, however, it's helpful to get down a few more basics. That way you'll better appreciate why this particular Apple is so yummy.

Navigating the Mac Desktop

All roads lead to and depart from the computer's *desktop,* the area that takes over your entire computer screen. On a PC, this is known as the Windows desktop. On a Macintosh, it's the Mac desktop or (as homage to the machine's operating system) the Snow Leopard desktop.

Indeed, the desktop is a launch pad for all that you may do on your computer. It is the scenic landscape upon which you organize and store things. Have a peek at Figure 3-1, which shows a typical Mac desktop layout.

Menu bar   Desktop   Hard drive icon

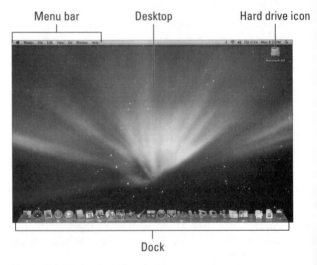

Dock

Figure 3-1: The typical Mac desktop.

The time is displayed near the upper-right corner of the screen, and a trash can is at the bottom right.

Look around and you'll see other funky-looking graphical icons on the screen.

Clicking the Menu Bar

See the narrow strip extending across the top of the desktop? Yes, the one with the little picture of an apple at the extreme left, and words such as File, Edit, and View to its right? This is your *menu bar,* so-named because clicking the apple — or any of the words in the strip — brings up a *menu,* or list of commands.

Single-click the apple, and a menu pops up with some important functions. The menu is so relevant that it is available from any application you're working in.

Understanding Icons, Folders, and Windows

Icons are the cutesy pictures that miraculously cause things to happen when you double-click them. Try double-clicking the icon labeled Macintosh HD in the upper-right corner of the desktop. The *HD* stands for hard drive. A window containing more icons appears. These represent the various software applications loaded on your hard drive, plus *folders* stuffed with files and documents.

Now try this one out for size: Double-click the Users folder. See whether you can locate your *home folder.* *Hint:* It's the one with a picture of a house and your name. Double-click the home folder, and yet another window jumps to the forefront. It contains *subfolders* for the documents you have created, plus movies, music, and pictures.

The windows on the Mac can be stretched, dragged to a new locale on the desktop, and laid one on top of another. To help you understand Mac windows, check out Figure 3-2. The *sidebar,* on the left, is a list of frequently used folders, programs, and other items, grouped into categories. You click the toolbar button to hide or show the toolbar and sidebar.

Close, minimize, zoom window

Next and previous window

View as icons, list, columns, Cover Flow

Quick Look/Slideshow   Search

Click for menu   Toolbar button

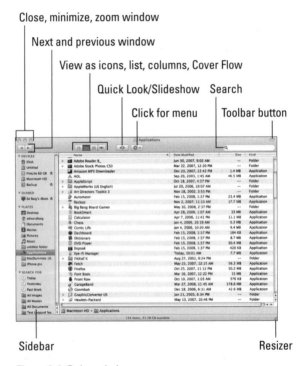

Sidebar   Resizer

Figure 3-2: Doing windows.

A stunning view

The Mac graciously lets you view information from four perspectives. Open the View menu in the menu bar and choose As icons, As list, As columns, or As Cover Flow (or click one of the buttons labeled in Figure 3-2).

Have a Quick Look

Apple gives the Snow Leopard crowd yet another clever way to peek at the contents of files on your Mac — without having to launch the applications that created those files. More than living up to its moniker, *Quick Look* lets you look at a file as a pretty decent-sized thumbnail or even full-screen. And Quick Look could also be called Quick Listen because you can even play music. Indeed, the feature works with all sorts of files — PDFs, spreadsheets, Microsoft Word documents, movies, and more.

Here's how to make it happen:

1. **Highlight a file.**

2. **Click the Quick Look button (labeled in Figure 3-2) or press the spacebar.**

   The file jumps out at you in a window. To display the file full-screen, click the button that looks like two diagonal arrows pointing in opposite directions.

3. **If you're looking at a picture and want to add it to your iPhoto image library, click the iPhoto button.**

4. **If you decide to open the file you're previewing and the program that opens it, double-click Quick Look preview.**

You can preview multiple images in Quick Look.
Just highlight more than one file and press the
Quick Look toolbar button or the spacebar.
Then use the forward or backward arrow to
navigate through the files. Or press play for a
slideshow.

What's Up, Dock?

Your eyes can't help but be drawn to the colorful
reflective three-dimensional bar at the bottom of the
screen (refer to Figure 3-1). This is your *dock*. It may
comfort those familiar with Microsoft's way of designing a computer interface to think of the dock as a
rough cross between the Windows taskbar and the
Start menu. In my humble opinion, it's more attractive
than the Windows taskbar. More fun too.

The dock is divided into two parts by a white dashed
line. To the left of the line are programs and other
tools. To the right are any open files and folders, plus
a collection of expandable icons called *Stacks*. (Stacks
are collections of icons to keep your desktop organized and tidy, especially when downloading files; see
the next section for more on Stacks.) You'll also find
the trash can.

Here are a few things to remember about the dock:

   ✔ To launch a program or other activity, single-
      click a dock icon. In most other places, you have
      to double-click an icon to make it get off its
      derrière.

   ✔ To see the name of the program that an icon
      represents, mouse over the icon on the dock.

   ✔ The appearance of a shiny orb below an icon
      means the program is open.

> ✔ To add an icon to the dock, drag it there.
>
> ✔ To remove an icon from the dock, drag it away.
>
> ✔ You can alter the size of the dock by clicking the dashed line and dragging it to the left or right.

Stockpiling Stacks

A handy Snow Leopard feature called Stacks brings another organizational tool to your desktop. Stacks are simply a collection of files organized by theme, and they do wonders for all you clutterholics in the crowd, of which, alas, I am one. You'll find Stacks to the right of the dashed divider on the dock.

Apple has already put together two useful premade Stacks right off the bat. One is a Stack for your documents; the other is reserved for all the stuff you might download — such as saved Mail attachments, file transfers through iChat, and files captured from the Internet with the Safari browser.

I'm fond of the Downloads Stack, which bobs up and down to let you know a new arrival is there. The icon for the Downloads Stack takes the form of the most recent item you've downloaded, such as a PowerPoint presentation or an Audible audio file.

To view the contents of a Stack, click the Stacks icon. It immediately opens in one of two ways: Icons for the files, along with their names, fan out in an arc (see Figure 3-3), or files and names appear as a grid. You can dictate whether Stacks spring out as a fan or a grid. Right-click or Control-click the Stacks icon on the dock to instantly bring up the Stack's *contextual menu* and make your choice.

Figure 3-3: Fanning out your files.

You can turn any folder in your arsenal into a Stack
by dragging it from the desktop to the right of the
dock's dashed line and to the left of the trash.

A Gaggle of Freebie Programs

A major fringe benefit of Mac ownership is all the nifty
software you get gratis. Many of these freebie programs are part of iLife. The programs listed here,
however, are of smaller stature. I'm not demeaning
them; many are handy to have around:

- ✔ **Address Book** is a handy repository
  for addresses, phone numbers, and e-mail
  addresses.

- ✔ The Mac has **three calculators:** basic, scientific,
  and programmer.

- ✔ The Mac supplies versions of the *New Oxford
  American Dictionary* and *Oxford American
  Writer's Thesaurus*.

✔ **iCal,** Mac's personal calendar application, lets you share your calendar with people on the same computer, "publish" a calendar over the Internet to share with others, and subscribe to public calendars over the Internet.

✔ **iSync** keeps your calendar, Address Book, and Internet bookmarks synchronized across multiple devices, such as a cell phone, a PDA, and an iPod.

✔ **Preview** is a versatile program that lets you view graphics files and faxes, take screen shots, convert file formats, and handle PDFs with ease and style.

✔ **QuickTime,** the Mac's multimedia player, comes to the rescue when you want to watch a movie (but not a DVD), play sounds, and display pictures.

✔ **Stickies** are electronic Post-it notes. Like the gluey paper kind, Stickies let you jot down quickie shopping lists, phone numbers, and to-dos.

✔ The **TextEdit** word processor doesn't offer anywhere near the flexibility of, say, Microsoft Word, but it's no slouch either. You can create tables and lists and apply a bunch of formatting. And it can accommodate Word documents (if someone sends you one).

You'll find some of these programs on the dock. Another good place to look is the *Applications folder,* which is accessible by clicking Applications in the sidebar or choosing Go⇨Applications.

Chapter 4

Making the Mac Your Own

. . . .

In This Chapter

▶ Creating and ranking user accounts

▶ Implementing parental controls

▶ Logging on and off

▶ Personalizing your Mac's appearance

▶ Exposing Exposé

▶ Becoming a Spaces cadet

▶ Setting priorities

. . . .

*Y*ou adore your family and friends to death but have to admit that they get under your skin from time to time. They know how to push your buttons, and you sure know how to push theirs. People are fussy about certain things, and that includes you (and me).

So it goes with your Macintosh. The presumption is that you and your Mac are going to cohabit well into the future. Still, it can't hurt to get off on the right foot and set up the machine so that it matches your personal preferences and expectations, and not some programmer's at Apple. The software you load on

your system differs from the programs your best buddies install on their computers. You tolerate dozens
of icons on the Mac desktop; they prefer a less cluttered screen. You choose a blown-up picture of
Homer Simpson for your desktop background; your
pals go with a screen-size poster of Jessica Simpson.

Establishing User Accounts

As much as the computer staring you in the face is
your very own Mac, chances are you'll be sharing it
with someone else: your spouse and kids, perhaps, if
not your students and coworkers. I know you gener-
ously thought about buying each of them a computer.
But then your little one needs braces, you've been
eyeing a new set of golf clubs and, the truth is, your
largesse has limits. So you'll be sharing the computer,
all right, at least for awhile. The challenge now is
avoiding chaos and all-out civil war.

The Mac helps keep the peace by giving everyone
their own user accounts, which are separate areas to
hang out in that are password protected to prevent
intrusions. (There's not much the folks at Apple
can do to avert fights over *when* people use the
computer.)

Ranking user accounts

In Chapter 2, I explain how you create your own user
account as part of the initial computer setup. But not
all user accounts are created equal, and yours is extra
special. That's because as the owner of the machine,
you're the head honcho, the Big Cheese, or in the
bureaucracy of your computer, the *administrator.*

Being the Big Cheese doesn't earn you an expense
account or a plush corner office with a view of the

lakefront. It does, however, carry executive privileges. You get to lord over not only who else can use the machine but who, if anyone, gets the same administrative rights you have.

Think long and hard before you grant anyone else these dictatorial powers. Only an administrator can install new programs in the Applications folder, or muck around with system settings such as Date & Time and Energy Saver. And only an administrator can effectively hire and fire, by creating or eliminating other user accounts.

Let's take a quick look at the hierarchy of accounts:

- ✔ **Administrator:** As outlined previously, you have almighty powers, at least when it comes to your computer.

- ✔ **Standard:** You can't mess with other people's accounts. But you do pretty much have free reign when it comes to your own account. That means you can install software, alter the look of your desktop, and so on.

- ✔ **Managed with Parental Controls:** Consider this mom and dad's revenge. The kids may get away with murder around the house, but they can't get away with murder on the Mac.

- ✔ **Sharing Only:** A limited account for sharing files remotely across a network.

- ✔ **Group:** By creating a group account, you can share files with the members of said group. It's really a type of account comprised of one or more accounts.

- ✔ **Guest:** Willing to let the babysitter play with your Mac after putting the little ones to bed? A guest account lets her log in without a password (though you can still restrict her activities through parental controls). You can allow guests to connect to shared folders on the system. Or not. And the beauty of one of these accounts is that once a guest has logged out, all traces of her stay are removed, right down to the temporary home folder created for her visit.

Creating new accounts

So now that you know the different types of user accounts, let's find out more about setting up one. To create a new account for one of your coworkers, say, follow these steps:

1. Choose ⌘⇨System Preferences, and then click the Accounts icon in the System section.

2. If the Password tab isn't highlighted, click it.

3. Click the + on the lower left below the list of names.

4. In the screen that opens, do the following:

   a. In New Account pop-up menu, choose one of the account designations listed in the preceding section.

   b. Enter a name, a short name, a password, the password verification, and (if you choose) a password hint in the blank fields shown.

   c. Click Create Account.

Using Parental Controls: When Father (or Mother) Knows Best

Suppose one of the new accounts you create is for your impressionable offspring Cookie Monster. As a responsible parent, you want to set limits to keep him out of trouble. And as a responsible Mac owner, you want to keep him from unwittingly or (or otherwise) inflicting damage on the computer.

It's time to apply *parental controls.* Presumably, you already set up Cookie Monster as a managed account with parental controls. If not, click to select the Enable Parental Controls box in the Accounts window. When you do so, Cookie Monster's account goes from being a regular standard account to a managed account, with you as the manager. You have quite a bit of say about what your youngster can and cannot get away with. Let's have a look.

In the Accounts window, click Open Parental Controls. Alternatively click Parental Controls inside System Preferences. Either way you'll end up in the same place. In the Parental Controls window, shown in Figure 4-1, select Cookie Monster's name in the list on the left. Now, protective parent, there's lots you can do.

Let's dive in to the five tabs at the top of the window:

- ✔ **System:** Parents can select the Use Simple Finder box to provide Cookie Monster with the most restricted barebones desktop. Only three folders reside in the Simple Finder version of the Dock (My Applications, Documents, and Shared). Meanwhile, the only applications your kid gets to see are those you've designated by selecting the Only Allow Selected Applications option. In this System view, you can also choose whether the little guy can administer printers, burn CDs and DVDs, change a password, and modify the Dock. (Dock modification is categorically disallowed in Simple Finder.)

- ✔ **Content:** By selecting this tab, you can filter out four-letter words in Dictonary. You can also restrict Web access so that all Cookie Monster supposedly gets to see are clean sites. Apple will make the decision on your behalf if you select the Try to Limit Access to Adult Website Automatically option. If you click Customize, you can list your own approved sites, as well as

those you don't deem kosher. To see some of
the sites that meet Apple's approval, click Allow
Access to Only These Websites. Discovery Kids,
PBS Kids, and Smithsonian Institution are
among the sites that made Apple's list.

Figure 4-1: Parental controls may protect your kid and your
computer.

✔ **Mail & iChat:** By selecting Limit Mail and/or
Limit iChat, you get to approve who Cookie
Monster can exchange e-mails and hold chats
with through instant messages. You can also
receive an e-mail permission request should
Cookie Monster attempt to communicate with
someone who isn't on the A-OK list.

✔ **Time Limits:** It's not only a matter of who Cookie Monster would like to interact with or what programs he wants to play around with — it's also a matter of when you let him do so. By dragging the sliders shown in Figure 4-2, you can establish weekday and weekend time restrictions. In other words, you can prevent access to the Mac when it's time for him to go beddy-bye, choosing different times on school nights and weekends. Cookie Monster will get a fair warning shortly before shut down time so he can save his work. He'll also get the opportunity to plead for more time.

✔ **Logs:** We know you trust your child. Honest. All the same, you want to make sure he's safe and sound. So here's where you get to, um, monitor (that's the nice way of saying it) his behavior. You can to see the Web sites he visited or tried to visit), the applications he used, and who he chatted with. You can log activity for one week, one month, three months, and so on. And you can group logs by contact or date.

You don't have to have kids to implement parental controls. These controls work nicely in setting limits on employees, friends, or visiting relatives.

Is your kid using another Mac in the house? You can remotely manage parental controls across all the Macs in your home network. You'll have to set up an administrator account across all the computers you want to manage. In the lower-left corner of the Parental Controls window, click the small gear icon (just above the padlock). From the pop-up menu, select Allow Remote Setup. Repeat this exercise on each Mac you want to manage.

Figure 4-2: Time's up: Placing stringent limits on junior.

The Lowdown on Logging On and Off

You can create user accounts for any and all family members or visitors who will be using a particular Mac. And you can control how they log in. In this section I describe how.

In System Preferences, choose Accounts Preferences, and then click Login Options at the bottom of the left pane, under the list of all the account holders on your system. If need be, click the padlock and enter a name

and administrative password. Once in, you'll see the
window shown in Figure 4-3.

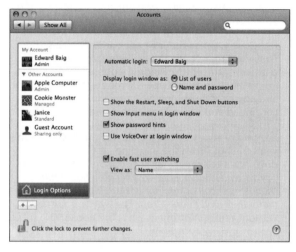

Figure 4-3: Choosing login options.

To automatically log in a particular user (likely yourself), select the Automatic Login option and choose
the appropriate person from the pop-up menu. You'll
have to enter a password.

 If the computer is set to automatically log you
in, any user who restarts the Mac in your
absence will have access to your account.

If automatic login is not turned on, users who start
the Mac will encounter the computer's Login screen.
It will appear differently depending on which radio
button you chose under Display Login Window As
under Login Options.

Select List of Users to see a Login screen with a roster of people alongside pictures for their respective accounts. Select Name and Password, and account holders must type a user name and password in the appropriate boxes on the Login screen.

Either way, press Enter or click after entering the password to actually log in. If you type the wrong password, the entire window wobbles as if having a momentary seizure. Type it wrong a few more times, and any password hints you previously entered appear (provided you chose that option under Login Options).

Say you're ready to call it quits for the day but don't want to shut down the machine. At the same time, you don't want to leave your account open for anyone with prying eyes. *Baig's Law: Just because your family, friends, and coworkers are upstanding citizens doesn't mean they won't eavesdrop.* The way to shut down without really shutting down is to choose ⇨Log Out.

Changing Appearances

Now that you've played boss of the system, you can get back in touch with your kinder, gentler side — the part of you solely occupied with making the Mac look pretty.

Altering buttons and the desktop

Are you not keen on the look of buttons, menus, and windows on your Mac? Is the wallpaper that Apple's interior designers put behind your desktop attractive enough but not your taste? You can rip it down and start anew.

Choose ⇨System Preferences and then click Appearance. This is where you can alter the menus and the color of those buttons, and apply other cosmetic touches.

Then move on to the Desktop & Screen Saver System Preference to really start putting your stamp on the place. Make sure the Desktop tab is highlighted, as shown in Figure 4-4. Click one of the design categories in the list on the left (Apple Images, Nature, Plants, and so on). Various design swatches appear on the right. Best of all, unlike the swatches a salesperson might show you in a home decorating store, you can see what a finished remodeling job here will look like. All you have to do is click.

Figure 4-4: Becoming your own interior decorator.

The design categories on the left include a listing for the Pictures Folder as well as albums from your iPhoto library. Clicking these options lets you choose one of your own images for the desktop background. Apple's designer collection has nothing over master-pieces that include your gorgeous child.

If variety is the spice of life — or you have a short attention span — click to add a check mark to the Change Picture Every 30 Minutes option (or select another timeframe from the pop-up menu). Selecting the Random Order option will (you guessed it) change the background in random order. This option cycles through pictures in the folder selected in the left pane.

While you're at it, click to select or deselect the Translucent Menu Bar box depending on your fancy.

Choosing a screen saver

"God save the screen. God save the screen? What's that, wrong slogan? Queen? Oh, royal bummer, never mind."

Screen savers are so-named because they were created to save your screen from a ghostly phenomenon known as burn-in. Whenever the same fixed image was shown on a screen over long periods of time, a dim specter from that image would be permanently etched onto the display. Burn-in isn't much of an issue anymore, but screen savers survived. Today their value is strictly cosmetic, in the same way you might choose a vanity license plate or a ring tone for your cell phone.

In the Desktop & Screen Saver pane of System Preferences click the Screen Saver tab. (Not there? Choose ➔System Preferences and then click Desktop & Screen Saver.)

Click one of the screen savers in the box on the left, as shown in Figure 4-5. Some of the pictures are stunning. (I recommend Cosmos or Nature Patterns.) You can also select images from your own photo

library or install screen savers created by companies other than Apple.

 If you want to know what words such as "*sopo-
rific*" or "*flume*" mean, choose the Word of the
Day screen saver. It's not as pretty as some
other options, but at least it'll boost your
vocabulary.

You can preview screen savers in the small screen to
the right or click the Test button to get the full-screen
effect.

After choosing a screen saver (or again having Apple
choose one for you randomly), drag the Start Screen
Saver slider to tell the Mac to choose a time for the
screen saver to kick in, ranging from three minutes to
two hours (or never).

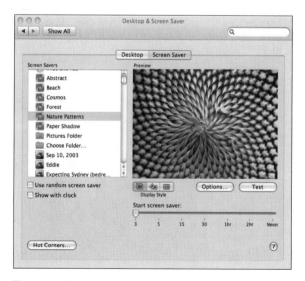

Figure 4-5: Beautifying your display with a screen saver.

Tidying Up with Exposé

You are so frantically busy that your papers end up strewn every which way, empty coffee cups litter your desk, and boxes pile on top of boxes. Worse, you can't lay your hands on the precise thing you need the very moment when you need it. Sound familiar? Psychiatrists have a technical name for this kind of disorder. It is called being a slob. (Takes one to know one.)

Things can get untidy on the Mac desktop, too, especially as you juggle several projects at once. At any given time, you may have opened System Preferences, Dictionary, iCal, an e-mail program, numerous word processing documents, and then some. Windows lay on top of windows. Chaos abounds. You have fallen into the dark abyss that is multitasking.

Apple has the perfect tonic for MDLS (Messy Desktop Layered Syndrome), shown in Figure 4-6. The antidote is *Exposé,* and it is as close as your F9 key (or the fn+F9 combination on some models).

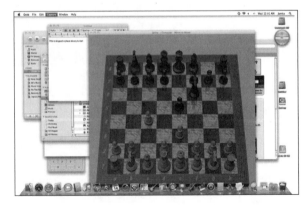

Figure 4-6: A cluttered desktop before putting Exposé to work.

Go ahead and press F9 (or fn + F9) now (or F3 on Apple's new aluminum keyboard). Each previously open but obstructed window emerges from its hiding place, like crooks finally willing to give themselves up after a lengthy standoff. All the windows are proportionately and simultaneously downsized so that you can temporarily see them all at once, as shown in Figure 4-7.

Figure 4-7: Exposé in action.

Now move the cursor over one of the visible windows. The title of the application or folder is revealed, and the window appears dimmed. Point to the window you want to bring to the front (to work on) and press the spacebar, or press Enter, or click inside the window.

Exposé is good for a few other stunts, and these are the default keys to make them happen:

> ✔ **F10 (or ⌘+F3 on the new keyboard):** Opens all the windows in the application you're currently using. If you're working on a document in

TextEdit, for instance, any other open documents in the program will also be brought to the
front lines.

✔ **F11 (or ⌘+F3 on the new keyboard):** Hides all
windows so you can admire the stunning photo-
graph you chose for your desktop.

If you have something against F9, F10, and F11 (or
other keys you're using for Exposé), open System
Preferences, choose Exposé & Spaces, and assign
alternative keys. And if you have something against
keys in general, you can arrange to have Exposé do its
thing by moving the cursor to one of the four corners
of the screen.

Incidentally, if you're wondering about the Spaces
part of Exposé & Spaces, read on. Then we'll close
this chapter with a tour of some of the remaining
items in System Preferences.

Getting Spaced Out

Exposé is terrific for reducing clutter. But it can't solve
one basic organizational problem: keeping only those
programs and windows related to a distinct pastime in
one dedicated location. That's where the Leopard feature known as Spaces comes in. It lets you display only
the stuff required to tackle the projects at hand.

So maybe you're an e-mailin' Web surfin' kind of dude.
Maybe you're putting together a family scrapbook.
And maybe you're writing a *For Dummies* book in
your spare time. You can set up separate spaces for
each of these activities. Here's how:

1. **In System Preferences, click Exposé & Spaces.**

2. **Make sure the Spaces tab is selected, as shown
   in Figure 4-8.**

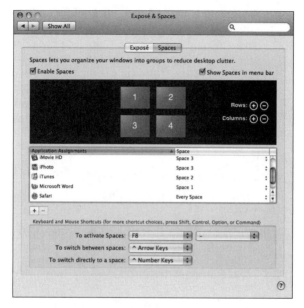

Figure 4-8: Organizing Spaces.

---

3. **Click Enable Spaces.**

4. **Click Show Spaces in Menu Bar.**

   Okay, in truth this step is optional. But it's a
   handy way to keep track of what space you're in.

5. **Click the + and – buttons next to Rows and
   Columns to select the number of Spaces you
   think you will need and configure their layout.**

   You can choose between a two-Spaces layout and
   sixteen-by-sixteen grid, with each one numbered,
   up to the total sum of spaces you've selected.

6. **To assign particular applications to specific
   spaces, click the + under the Applications**

> **Assignments list and then click under Space to choose the one you have in mind.**

That e-mailin' surfin' dude would likely add the Mac's Mail programs and the Safari browser to a particular Space. The family scrapbooker would probably put iPhoto to work in another.

Choose Every Space if you want an application to be available no matter what space you're in, as I do with the Safari Web browser.

Moving from space to space

Discovering a few key moves will turn you into a real space cadet.

- ✔ To view all your spaces at once, as shown in Figure 4-9, press the F8 key on your keyboard. Just click on a space to enter. You can drag spaces around this bird's-eye view to reorder them.

- ✔ To go directly to a space, press the Ctrl and the number key of the Space you want to drop in on.

- ✔ To move to the next or last space, press Ctrl and the left or right navigation arrow key, respectively.

- ✔ If you chose Show Spaces in Menu Bar as outlined in the preceding steps, click the Spaces icon in the menu bar and click the space you want to go to.

- ✔ If an application is assigned to a specific space, opening it on the dock will automatically transport you to that space.

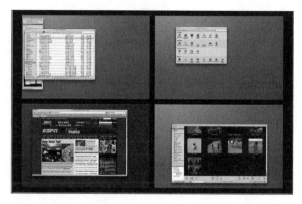

Figure 4-9: A bird's-eye view of Spaces.

 As clutter-fighting agents, Exposé and Spaces work well together. So from the birds-eye F8 view of Spaces, press the Exposé F9 key on (older) keyboards and watch as the open windows in each Space line up obediently. To return them to their previous position, press F9 again.

 When you enable Spaces (or Exposé, and so on) to override a hard-coded function on the newer Apple keyboard, you can always go back to it using the fn key. For example, if you have the Spaces full view set for F8 but you wanted to use play/pause, you would simply press fn and F8 to get that functionality.

Moving windows between spaces

Maybe you decide that a particular window is better suited to a different space, at least for the moment. Try these tricks.

> ✔ From the bird's-eye view, merely drag a window from one space to another.
>
> ✔ If you're already working in a space, drag the window you want to move to the left or right edge of the screen while holding down the mouse. A moment later the window will switch to the adjacent space.
>
> ✔ You may need to be an athlete to pull this one off. But here are Apple's own instructions. "Move the pointer over the window, and hold down the mouse button while pressing the Ctrl key and an arrow or number key."

System Preferences: Choosing Priorities

You may be wondering what's left. We've already created user accounts and ranked them, made logging on and off settings, and dug inside System Preferences to alter the desktop and screen saver. But as Figure 4-10 shows, you can still do a lot more. Let's explore some of these options now and some later.

Getting in sync with date and time

You established the date, time, and time zone when you set up the Mac initially (see Chapter 2). In System Preferences, you can move the location of the clock from the menu bar to a separate window. You can change the appearance of the clock from a digital readout to an analog face with hands. If you choose a digital clock, you can flash the time separators — or not. You can display the time with seconds use a twenty-four-hour clock or both. You can even have the Mac announce the time on the hour, the half hour, or the quarter hour.

Figure 4-10: Doing it my way through System Preferences.

Displays

If you are hunky-dory with what your display looks like, feel free to ignore this section. Read on if you're the least bit curious about *resolution* and what changing it will do to your screen. Resolution is a measure of sharpness and is expressed by tiny picture elements, or *pixels*. Pixels is such a nice sounding word that I always thought it would make a terrific name for a breakfast cereal, something like new Kellogg's *Sugar-Coated Pixels*. But I digress.

You'll see resolution written out as 800 x 600, 1024 x 768, 1680 x 1050, and so on. The first number refers to the number of pixels horizontally, and the second number is the number of pixels vertically. Higher numbers reflect higher resolution, meaning the picture is sharper and you can fit more on the screen. At lower resolutions the images may be larger but fuzzier, though this depends on your monitor, and any resolution other than the native one on an LCD display will be somewhat fuzzy. Lower resolutions also *refresh,* or update, more quickly, though you'll be hard-pressed to tell with most modern monitors. As it happens, the refresh rate doesn't mean boo on computers such as iMacs with LCD or flat-panel displays.

You can also play around with the number of colors that a Mac displays (millions, thousands, or down to a puny 256). Best advice: Play around with these settings if you must. More often than not, leave well enough alone.

Sound

Ever wonder what the *Basso* sound is? Or *Sosumi* or *Tink?* I'd play them for you if this was an audio book, but because it isn't, check out these and other sound effects in System Preferences. You'll hear one of them whenever the Mac wants to issue an alert. Sound Preferences is also the place to adjust speaker balance, microphone settings, and pretty much anything else having to do with what you hear on the Mac.

Software update

Your Mac may be a machine, but it still has organic traits. And Apple hasn't forgotten about you just because you've already purchased one of its prized computers. From time to time, the company will issue new releases of certain programs to add features it won't make you pay for, to *patch* or fix bugs, or to thwart security threats. For a full log, click Installed Updates.

You can have the Mac check for automatic software updates daily (might be overkill), weekly, monthly, or on the spot. If you choose, the Mac will fetch important updates in the background, and bother you only when the program update is ready to be installed.

Software Update is accessible also directly from the
 menu.

Universal Access

Some physically challenged users may require special
help controlling the Mac. Choose Universal Access
under System Preferences, and click the tab you need
assistance with: Seeing, Hearing, Keyboard, or Mouse,
as shown in Figure 4-11.

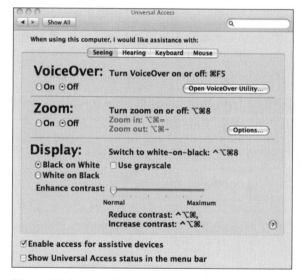

Figure 4-11: Universal Access preferences.

Among the options, you can arrange to

> ✔ Turn VoiceOver on or off, to hear descriptions
> of what's on your screen. And by opening the
> VoiceOver utility, you can change the default

voice. With Snow Leopard, VoiceOver supports the most popular Braille displays.

✔ Enhance the contrast, or alter the display from black on white or white on black.

✔ Flash the screen when an alert sound occurs.

✔ Zoom in on the screen to make everything appear larger. Or enlarge the size of the pointer if you have trouble seeing the mouse.

✔ Use a Slow Keys function to put a delay between when a key is pressed and when the result of that keypress is accepted. Or, if you can't easily press several keys at once, use Sticky Keys to press groups of modifier keys (Shift, ⌘, Option, and Control) in a sequence.

The Mac may share a nickname with a certain McDonald's hamburger. But it's actually an old Burger King slogan that is most apt when describing your computer. As this chapter has shown, you can "have it your way."

Chapter 5

Handling All That Busy Work

* *

In This Chapter

▶ Preparing your documents

▶ Selecting text

▶ Dragging, dropping, cutting, and pasting

▶ Switching the font

▶ Formatting documents

▶ Saving your work

▶ Making revisions

▶ Taking out the trash

▶ Hooking up a printer and printing

* *

*I*n professional football, the skill position players —
quarterback, running backs, and wide receivers —
get a disproportionate amount of the glory when a
team wins and assume most of the blame when they
fall on their collective fannies. But any halfway-
competent field general will tell you that those in
the trenches typically determine the outcome.

Sure you want to draw up a razzamatazz game plan
for your Mac. Probably something involving

stupendous graphics and spine-tingling special effects. A high-tech flea-flicker, to keep it in the grid-iron vernacular.

After all, you bought the computer with the intention of becoming the next Mozart, Picasso, or at the very least Steve Jobs. (*What, you expected Peyton or Eli Manning?*)

But for this one itty-bitty chapter, I am asking you to keep your expectations in check. You have to make first downs before you make touchdowns. Forget heaving Hail Mary's down the field. You're better off grinding out yardage the tough way.

In coach-speak, the mission of the moment is to master the computing equivalent of blocking and tackling: basic word processing and the other fundamentals required to get you through your daily routine.

Practice these now. You can pour the Gatorade on my head later.

Form and Function: The Essentials of Word Processing

I'm old enough to recall life before word processors. (Hey it wasn't *that* long ago.)

> I can't possibly begin to fathom how we survived in the days before every last one of us had access to word processors and computers on our respective desks.

Pardon the interruption, but I'm not thrilled with the preceding sentence. Kind of wordy and repetitious. Permit me to get right to the point.

I can't imagine how any of us got along without word processors.

Thanks, much more concise.

The purpose of this mini-editing exercise is to illustrate the splendor of word processing. Had I produced these sentences on a typewriter instead of a computer, changing even a few words would hardly seem worth it. I would have to use correction fluid to erase my previous comments and type over them. If things got really messy, or I wanted to take my writing in a different direction, I'd end up yanking the sheet of paper from the typewriter in disgust and begin pecking away anew on a blank page.

Word processing lets you substitute words at will, move entire blocks of text around with panache, and display characters in various typefaces or using specific fonts. You won't even take a productivity hit swapping typewriter ribbons (or swapping out balls) in the middle of a project, though you will at some point have to replace the ink in your printer.

 Before running out to buy Microsoft Word (or another industrial-strength and expensive) word processing program for your Mac — and I'm not suggesting you don't — it's my obligation to point out that Apple includes a respectable word processor with OS X. The program is *TextEdit,* and it calls the Applications folder home. TextEdit will be our classroom for much of this chapter.

Creating a Document

The first order of business using TextEdit (or pretty much any word processor) is to create a new *document*. There's really not much to it. It's about as easy as opening the program itself. The moment you do so, a window with a large blank area on which to type appears, as Figure 5-1 shows.

Figure 5-1: In the beginning was a blank page.

Have a look around the window. At top you see
Untitled because no one at Apple is presumptuous
enough to come up with a name for your yet-to-be-
produced manuscript. We'll get around to naming
(and saving) your stuff later. In my experience it helps
to write first and add a title later, though, um, schol-
ars may disagree.

Notice the blinking vertical line at the upper-left edge
of the screen, just below the ruler. That line, called
the *insertion point,* might as well be tapping out Morse
code for "start typing here."

Indeed, friends, you have come to the most challeng-
ing point in the entire word processing experience,
and believe me it has nothing to do with technology.
The burden is on you to produce clever, witty, and
inventive prose, lest all that blank space go to waste.

Okay, get it? At the blinking insertion point, type with
abandon. Something original like

   It was a dark and stormy night

If you type like I do, you may have accidentally
produced

   It was a drk and stormy nihgt

Fortunately, your amiable word processor has your
best interests at heart. See the dotted red line below
drk and *nihgt* in Figure 5-2? That's TextEdit's not-so-
subtle way of flagging a likely typo. (This presumes
you've left the default Check Spelling As You Type
activated in TextEdit Preferences. Since we're at the
beginning of this exercise, that seems like a safe
presumption.)

Figure 5-2: Oops, I made a mistake.

You can address these snafus in several ways. You can use the computer's Delete key to wipe out all the letters to the left of the insertion point. (Delete functions like the backspace key on the Smith Corona you put out to pasture years ago.) After the misspelled word has been quietly sent to Siberia, you can type over the space more carefully. All traces of your sloppiness disappear.

Delete is a wonderfully handy key. I'd recommend using it to eliminate a single word such as *nihgt.* But in our little case study, we have to repair *drk* too. And using Delete to erase *drk* means sacrificing *and* and *stormy* as well. Kind of overkill if you ask me.

Back to football. It's time to call an audible. A few quick options:

✔ Use the left-facing arrow key (found on the lower-right side of the keyboard) to move the insertion point to the spot just to the right of the word you want to deep-six. No characters are eliminated when you move the insertion point that way. Only when the insertion point is where it ought to be do you again hire your reliable keyboard hit-man, Delete.

✔ Eschew the keyboard and click with the mouse to reach this same spot to the right of the misspelled word. Then press Delete.

✔ Of course you need not delete anything. You can merely place the insertion point after the *d* and type an *a*.

Now try this helpful remedy. Right-click anywhere on the misspelled word. A list appears with suggestions, as shown in Figure 5-3. Single-click the correct word and, voila, it instantly replaces the mistake. Be careful in this example not to choose *dork*.

Figure 5-3: I'm no dork. I fixed it.

Selecting Text in a Document

Let's try another experiment. Double-click a word. See what happens. It's as if you ran a light-blue marker across the word. You've *highlighted,* or *selected,* this word so that it can be deleted, moved, or changed.

Many times, you'll want to select more than a single word. Perhaps a complete sentence. Or a paragraph. Or several paragraphs. Here's how to highlight a block of text to delete it:

1. **Using the mouse, point to the block in question.**

2. **Press and hold down the left mouse button and drag the cursor (which bears a slight resemblance to the Seattle Space Needle) across the entire section you want to highlight.**

   The direction in which you drag the mouse affects what gets highlighted. If you drag horizontally, a single line is selected. Dragging vertically selects an entire block. You can highlight text also by holding down Shift and using the arrow keys.

3. **Release the mouse button when you reach the end of the passage you want highlighted, as shown with *Once upon a time* in Figure 5-4.**

4. **To immediately wipe out the selected text, press Delete.**

   Alternatively, start typing. Your old material is exorcised upon your very first keystroke and replaced with the new characters you type.

To jump to a specific line of text, choose Edit⇨ Find⇨Select Line. Then enter its line number. Or to jump ahead, say, five lines, add the + symbol as in +5. To jump backward 5 lines, enter -5 instead.

Figure 5-4: Highlighting text.

To select several pages of text at once, single-click at the beginning portion of the material you want to select, and then scroll to the very bottom. While holding down the Shift key, click again. Everything between clicks is highlighted.

 Now suppose you were overzealous and selected too much text. Or maybe you released the mouse a bit too soon so that not enough of the passage you have in mind was highlighted. Just click once with your mouse to deselect the selected area and try again.

Another screw-up. This time you annihilated text that upon further review you want to keep. Fortunately, the Mac lets you perform a do-over. Choose Edit⇨

Undo Typing. The text is miraculously revived.
Variations of this lifesaving Undo command can be
found in most of the Mac programs you encounter. So
before losing sleep over some silly thing you did on
the computer, visit the Edit menu and check out your
Undo options.

Dragging and Dropping

In Chapter 3 I mention *dragging and dropping* to move
icons to the dock. In this chapter, we drag an entire
block of text to a new location and leave it there.

Select a passage in one of the ways mentioned in the
preceding section. Now, anywhere on the highlighted
area, click and hold down the mouse button. Roll the
mouse across a flat surface to drag the text to its new
destination. Release the mouse button to drop off the
text. And if you hold down the Option key, you can
drag a copy, which allows you to duplicate a passage
without having to cut and paste (see the next section).

You are not restricted to dragging and dropping text
in the program you're in. You can lift text completely
out of TextEdit and into Word, Stickies, or Pages, an
Apple program for producing spiffy-looking newsletters and brochures.

Alternatively, if you know you'll want to use a text block
in another program at some point in the future — you
just don't know when — drop it directly onto the Mac
desktop (see Figure 5-5) and call upon it whenever
necessary. Text copied to the desktop will be shown as
an icon and named from text in the beginning of the
selection you copied. Moving text in this manner to an
external program or the desktop constitutes a Copy
command, not a Move command, so the lifted text
remains in the original source.

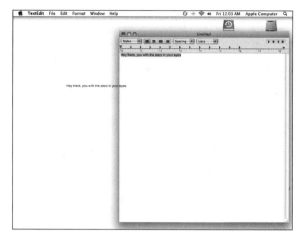

Figure 5-5: Dropping text on the desktop.

Cutting and Pasting

In the preceding section, we copied material from one location and moved a copy to another location. By contrast, cutting and pasting lifts material from one spot and moves it elsewhere without leaving anything behind. (In the typewriter era, you literally cut out passages of paper with scissors and pasted them onto new documents.)

After selecting your source material, choose Edit➪Cut (or the keyboard alternative ⌘+X). To paste to a new location, navigate and click the spot and choose Edit➪Paste (or ⌘+V).

The Cut command is easily confused with Copy (⌘+C). As the name suggests, the latter copies selected text that can be pasted somewhere else. Cut clips text out of its original spot.

The very last thing you copied or cut is temporarily sheltered on the clipboard. It remains there until replaced by newer material you copy or cut.

If you can't remember what you last placed on the clipboard, choose Edit⇨Show Clipboard when Finder (the leftmost dock icon) is activated.

Changing the Font

When typewriters were in vogue, you were usually pretty much limited to the typeface of the machine. Computers being computers, you can alter the appearance of individual characters and complete words effortlessly. Let's start with something simple.

In the TextEdit window, click the pop-up menu Styles and choose Italic. Highlighted text becomes *text.* Now try Bold. Highlighted text becomes **text.**

I recommend using keyboard shortcuts in this instance. Just before typing a word, try ⌘+I for *italics* or ⌘+B for *bold.* When you want to revert to normal type, just press those respective keyboard combinations again.

Making words bold or italic is the tip of the proverbial iceberg. You can dress up documents with different *fonts,* or typefaces.

Open the Format menu and choose Font⇨Show Fonts. A window appears where you can change the typeface of any highlighted text by clicking a font listed in the pane labeled Family. Choices carry names such as Arial, Baghdad, Chalkboard, Courier, Desdemona, Helvetica, Papyrus, Stencil, and Times New Roman.

Unless you wrote your graduate thesis on *Fontomology* (don't bother looking up the word; it's my invention), nobody on the *For Dummies* faculty expects you to have a clue about what any of the aforementioned fonts look like. I sure don't. Cheating is okay. Peek at your document to see how high-lighted words in the text change after clicking differ-ent font choices.

 As usual, another way to view different fonts is available. In the lower-left corner of the Font window, click the icon that looks like a gear or cog. Choose Show Preview from the menu (see Figure 5-6). You'll be able to inspect various font families and typefaces in the preview pane that appears above your selection. Click the gear icon again to choose Hide Preview.

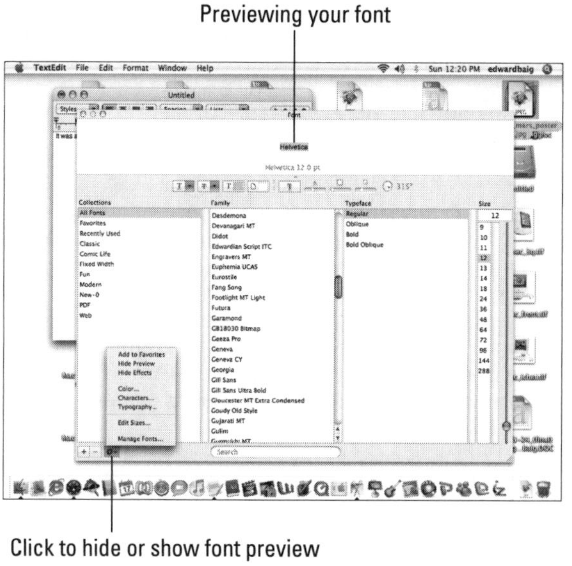

Previewing your font

![Screenshot of TextEdit Font window showing the font preview pane with Helvetica displayed, and a gear/cog menu open showing options including Add to Favorites, Hide Preview, Hide Effects, Color..., Characters..., Typography..., Edit Sizes..., Manage Fonts...]

Click to hide or show font preview

Figure 5-6: Previewing your fonts.

Formatting Your Document

Fancy fonts aren't the only way to doll up a document. You have important decisions to make about proper margins, paragraph indentations, and text tabs. And you must determine whether lines of text should be single or double-spaced. Hey it's still a lot easier than using a typewriter.

Okay, we're back in our TextEdit classroom. Set your margins and tab stops by dragging the tiny triangles along the ruler.

Now click the drop-down menu that says Spacing, just above the ruler. Clicking Single separates the lines in the way you are reading them in this paragraph.

If I go with Double, the line jumps down to here, and the next line

jumps down to here.

Got it?

The control freaks among you (you know who you are) might want to click Other under the Spacing menu. It displays the dialog box shown in Figure 5-7. Now you can precisely determine the height of your line, the way the paragraphs are spaced (that is, the distance from the bottom of a paragraph to the top of the first line in the paragraph below), and other parameters, according to the points system.

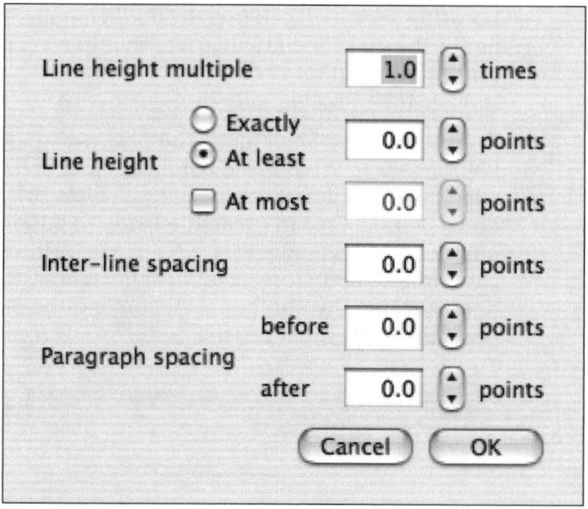

Figure 5-7: When it has to look just like this.

Here are other tricks that make TextEdit a capable writing companion:

- ✔ **Aligning paragraphs:** After clicking anywhere in a paragraph, choose Format⇨Text and choose an alignment (left, center, justified, or right). Play around with these choices to determine what looks best.

- ✔ **Writing from right to left:** I suppose this one's useful for writing in Hebrew or Arabic. Choose Format⇨Text⇨Writing Direction and then click Right to Left. Click again to go back the other way, or choose Edit⇨Undo Set Writing Direction.

✔ **Locating text:** You can use the Find command under the Edit menu to uncover multiple occurrences of specific words and phrases and replace them individually or collectively.

✔ **Producing lists:** Sometimes the best way to get your message across is in list form. Kind of like what I'm doing here. By clicking the Lists drop-down menu, you can present a list with bullets, numbers, roman numerals, uppercase or lowercase letters, and more, as shown in Figure 5-8. Keep clicking the choices until you find the one that makes the most sense.

Figure 5-8: Formatting a list.

✔ **Creating tables:** Then again, you may want to emphasize important points using a table or chart. Choose Format⇨Text⇨Table. In the window that appears (see Figure 5-9), you can select the number of rows and columns you need for your table. You can select a color background for each cell by clicking the Cell Background drop-down list and choosing Color Fill, and then choosing a hue from the palette that appears when you click the rectangle to the right. You can drag the borders of a row or a column to alter its dimensions. You can also merge or split table cells by selecting the appropriate cells and then clicking the Merge Cells or Split Cells button.

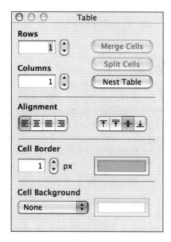

Figure 5-9: Creating a table.

✔ **Smart Quotes:** Publishers sometimes try to fancy up books by using curly quotation marks rather than straight ones. Somehow curly is smarter than straight. Whatever. To use smart quotes in the document you are working on, choose TextEdit⇨Edit⇨Substitutions⇨Smart Quotes. To use curly quotes in all docs, choose TextEdit Preferences, click New Document, and select the Smart Quotes box. If you've already selected smart quotes but want to revert to straight quotes inside some document you are working on, press Ctrl and apostrophe (for a single quotation mark) or Ctrl+Shift+apostrophe for a double quotation mark.

> ✓ **Smart Links:** You can set it up so that anytime
> you type an Internet address in a document, it
> acts as a link or jumping point to take you to that
> Web page. Choose TextEdit⇨Substitutions⇨
> Smart Links to use a smart link in the document
> you are working on. Or visit TextEdit Preferences,
> click New Document, and select the Smart Links
> box to make this feature permanent.

Saving Your Work

You've worked so darn hard making your document
read well and look nice that I'd hate to see all your
efforts go to waste. And yet in the cruel world of computers that's precisely what could happen if you don't
take a second to *save* your file. And a second is all it
takes to save a file — but you can lose everything just
as fast.

Stable as it is, the Mac is a machine for goodness
sakes and not immune to power failures or human foi-
bles. Odd as it may seem, even tech authors pound a
calamitous combination of keys from time to time.

All the work you've done so far exists in an ethereal
kind of way, as part of *temporary* memory. Don't let the
fact that you can see something on your computer
monitor fool you. If you shut down your computer, or
it unexpectedly crashes (it's been known to happen
even on Macs), any unsaved material will reside
nowhere but in another type of memory. Your own.

So where exactly do you save your work? Why on the
Save sheet of course (see Figure 5-10). It slides into
view from the top of your document when you press
the keyboard combo ⌘+S or choose File⇨Save.

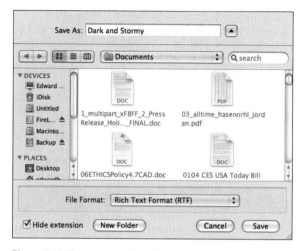

Figure 5-10: Everyone needs a file saver.

Remember way back in the beginning of this chapter
when I mentioned that Apple wouldn't dare name a
file for you (except to give it the temporary moniker
Untitled). Well this is your big chance to call the file
something special by filling in a title where it says
Save As. Go ahead and name it, I dunno, *Dark and
Stormy*.

When you click the Save button, the contents of Dark
and Stormy are assigned to a permanent home on
your Mac's hard drive, at least until you're ready to
work on the document again.

But there's more. You get to choose in which folder
to stash the file. The Mac suggests the Documents
folder, a logical choice. But you can choose among
several other possible destinations, as becomes clear

when you click the arrow next to where you just
named your document. You can stuff your manuscript
in any existing folder or subfolder in the sidebar or
create one from scratch by clicking the New Folder
button and giving the folder a name.

Snow Leopard in all wisdom provides a safety
net for saving. In other words, you can now save
TextEdit documents automatically. Choose
TextEdit⇨Preferences, and click Open and Save.
In the Autosave Modified Documents pop-up
menu, choose an appropriate time interval
(every 15 seconds, 30 seconds, minute, 5 minutes, or never).

Unless you take this last step, you are hereby
advised to save and save often as you work on
documents.

Making Revisions

Dark and Stormy is safe and sound on your hard
drive. But after downing a few chill pills overnight,
you have a brand-new outlook on life in the morning.
You're past your brooding period. You want to
rework your inspiration's central theme and give it a
new name too, *Bright and Sunny.*

Back to TextEdit we go.

Choose File⇨Open. A dialog box appears. Scroll down
in the folder where you last saved your document,
and double-click its name or icon when you find it.

You are now ready to apply your changes. Because
your document is only as permanent as the last time
you saved it, remember to save it early and often,
as you make revisions. (It's a good habit to get into
even if you've turned on the autosave preference:

TextEdit is not the only program in which you'll want to save your work, of course.) Along the way, you can rename your bestseller by using Save As and choosing a new name, though you'll still have the previous version under the old name.

You may be better off renaming a file by selecting it (from a Finder window or the desktop) and pressing Enter. Type the new name and press Enter again.

 As always, your Mac tries to assist you in these matters. The computer makes the assumption that if you worked on a document yesterday or the day before, you might want to take another stab at it today. And to prevent you, Oh Prolific One, from having to strain too hard digging for a document you may want to edit, choose File➪ Open Recent. Your freshest files will turn up in the list. Just click the name of the document you want to revisit.

Perhaps the fastest way to find a file you want to revise is to use the Spotlight tool. Choose Spotlight by single-clicking its icon at the upper-right corner of the screen and type the name of the manuscript that requires your attention.

Taking Out the Trash

Like much else in life, documents, if not entire folders, inevitably outlive their usefulness. The material grows stale. It takes on a virtual stench. It claims hard drive space you could put to good use elsewhere.

Yes it's time to take out the trash.

Use the mouse to drag the document's icon above the trash can in the dock. Release the mouse button when the trash can turns black.

As usual, there's a keyboard alternative, ⌘+Delete. Or you can choose File⇨Move to Trash.

You'll know you have stuff in the trash because the icon shows crumpled paper. And just like your real life trash bin, you'll want to completely empty it from time to time, lest your neighbors complain.

To do so, choose Empty Trash under the Finder menu or press ⌘+Shift+Delete. A warning will pop up (see Figure 5-11), reminding you that once your trash is gone, it is gone. (Even then you may be able to get it back by purchasing data recovery software or hiring an expert.)

If you're absolutely, positively certain that you want to get rid of the contents of your trash — and paranoid about industrial spies recovering the docs — choose Secure Empty Trash from the Finder menu instead of the regular Empty Trash command.

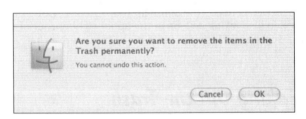

Are you sure you want to remove the items in the Trash permanently?

You cannot undo this action.

Cancel   OK

Figure 5-11: Think before trashing.

It's pretty easy to pull something out of the trash, provided you didn't take that last Draconian measure and select Empty Trash. It's less smelly or embarrassing than sticking your hands in a real trash bin. Click the Trash icon in the dock to peek at its contents. If you find

something worth saving after all, drag it back
onto the desktop or into the folder where it
used to reside.

Connecting and Activating a Printer

Almost all printers compatible with OS X, and that
includes most printers sold today, connect to your
Mac through the *Universal Serial Bus (USB)* port we
became acquainted with in Chapter 2. So much for un-
retiring the printer in the closet that connects
through what's called a *parallel* port.

You'll almost certainly leave the store considerably poorer than you would have first imagined
even with a bargain printer. *Gotta* buy stacks of
paper, extra ink because the starter cartridges
included with your printer may not last very
long, and very likely a USB cable.

The good news is not all printers require a cord.
Some are compatible with Wi-Fi or Bluetooth.

Ready, Set, Print

You have ink. You have paper. You have a USB cable.
You are antsy. Time's a wasting. I sense impatience.
Let's jump to the task at hand.

Plug the printer into an AC wall jack. Plug the USB
cable into the USB port on the Mac and make sure it's
connected snugly to the printer itself. Turn on your
printer. The thing is warmed and ready for action.
Snow Leopard big-heartedly assembled most of the
software *drivers* required to communicate with

modern printers. Chances are yours is one of them. If not, it probably resides on the software that came with the printer. Or visit the company's Web site.

Configuring wireless or wired (through Ethernet) net-worked printers is a tad more complicated. For now, we'll assume you've connected a USB printer. Open the Mac's trusted word processor, TextEdit. Then follow these steps:

1. **Open the document you want to print.**

2. **Choose File⇨Print, or use the keyboard short-cut ⌘+P.**

   Even though we're doing this exercise in TextEdit, you'll find the Print command under the File menu across your Mac software library. The ⌘+P shortcut works across the board too. The print window shown in Figure 5-12 appears. (If the print window that appears shows less than you see here, click the downward-pointing trian-gle at the upper right.)

3. **Click the Printer pop-up menu and select your printer, if available.**

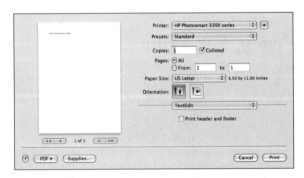

Figure 5-12: Fit to print?

4. **If your connected USB printer is not in the print window:**

   a. **Click Add Printer in the pop-up menu.**

      An add printer setup window opens.

   b. **If your printer appears in the list, click to select it (if it's not already selected). Click Add and you're golden. Continue with Step 5.**

   c. **If your printer isn't listed, click the printer connection type icon at the top and make the appropriate selection, as shown in Figure 5-13.**

      Choices include Default, Fax (if choosing a fax machine), IP (an Internet printer), AppleTalk (signifying a network), Bluetooth, and More Printers. When you make your choice, the Mac will search for any available printers.

   d. **Highlight the printer you want to use and then click Add.**

      You can alternatively click the Print Using pop-up menu and then choose Select a Driver to Use to find a specific model, if available.

5. **Choose from the bevy of options in the print window.**

   Select which pages to print. (All is the default, but you can give any range by tabbing from one From box to the other.) Click where indicated to select the paper size and print orientation, which you can examine in a quick preview of the document you want to print. You get to select the number of copies you need and whether you want pages collated. You can decide whether to print a header and footer. And you can choose whether to save your document in the Adobe PDF format (along with other PDF options).

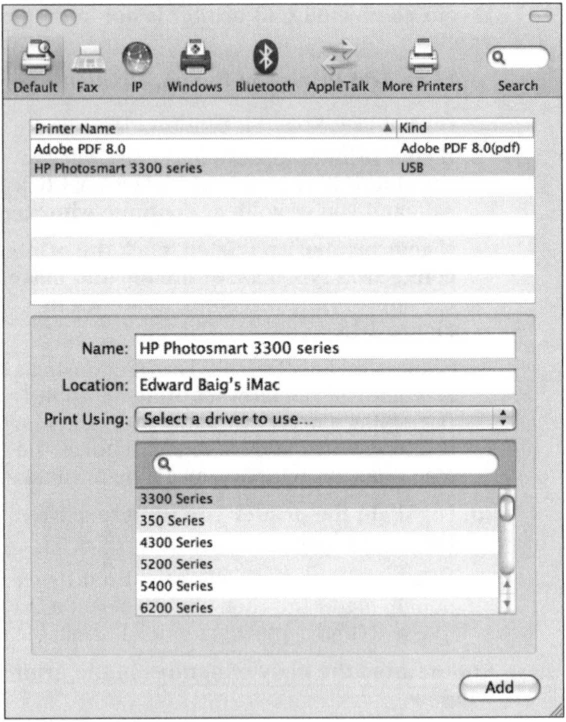

Figure 5-13: Adding a printer.

Note that this print window or dialog box differs a bit from program to program. In the Safari browser, for instance, you can choose whether or not to print backgrounds, an option that doesn't appear in the TextEdit dialog box.

6. **When you're satisfied with your selections, click Print.**

   If all goes according to plan, your printer will oblige.

Even if the Mac instantly recognizes your printer, I recommend loading any Mac installation discs that came with the printer.

Why bother? My printer is already printing stuff. The answer is that the disc might supply you with extra fonts, as well as useful software updates.

 It wouldn't hurt to also visit the printer manufacturer's Web site to see whether updated printer drivers are available.

Printing it your way

The Mac gives you a lot of control over how your printer will behave and your printouts will look.

You may have noticed another pop-up menu in the print sheet just below the orientation icons. TextEdit is now showing, but if you click the button, a gaggle of other choices present themselves. (Some listed options are specific to your printer or the application in use.)

✔ **Layout:** You can select the number of "pages" that will get printed on a single sheet of paper, and determine the ways those pages will be laid out, as shown in Figure 5-14. You can choose a page border (Single Thin Line, Double Hairline, and so on). And you can turn two-sided printing on or off, provided your printer can handle such a task.

✔ **Scheduler:** Suppose you have to print dozens of invitations for your spouse's surprise birthday party and want to make sure to do so when your honey is out of the house. Set your Mac to print at a time when the two of you are out together.

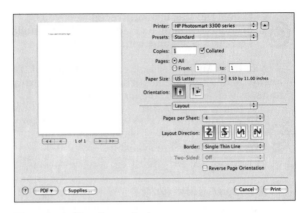

Figure 5-14: Choosing a print layout.

- ✔ **Paper Handling:** You can choose to print only odd- or even-numbered pages or to print pages in reverse order. You can also scale a page so that it fits a legal- or letter-sized sheet, an envelope, or a variety of other paper sizes.

- ✔ **Color Matching:** Choose this setting to select ColorSync Profiles (from Apple and others). Thus you can match the color on the screen to the color you are printing.

- ✔ **Cover Page:** Pretend you work for the CIA. Then print a cover sheet stating that everything else you're printing is classified, confidential, or top secret? (Yea, like they're not going to look.)

- ✔ **Paper Type/Quality:** Clues the printer in on the type of paper you loaded (inkjet, transparency film, brochure, and so on). You also get to choose the print quality. A fast draft uses less ink than printing in the spiffiest, or best, quality.

If your printer has more than one tray (for example, a main tray and a photo tray), you can also choose the source of the paper to use.

✔ **Borderless Printing:** Tell your printer to print without borders. Or not.

This seems as good a time as any to see what other print options await you in System Preferences, found per usual under the menu. In the Hardware section of System Preferences, click the Print & Fax icon. You can select the Share This Printer box if you are willing to share the printer with other computers in your house or office.

Now click the Print Queue button to check the status of any current printing jobs, among other things.

Previewing your print

Before you waste ink and paper on an ill-advised print job, you probably want to be sure your documents meet your lofty standards. That means the margins and spacing look jiffy and you have a clean layout with no *widows.* That's publishing-speak for a lonely word or two on a line of text all to itself.

As you've already seen, the Mac lets you sneak a peek in the small window that appears in the TextEdit (and other program's) print dialog. For a larger view in such programs as Microsoft Word, choose File⇨Print Preview.

If you're satisfied with the preview, go ahead and click Print. If not, go back and apply the necessary changes to your documents.

One more nice thing about printing on your Mac: The various programs you work in give you lots more custom printing options. For example, you can print a CD jewel case insert in iTunes or a pocket address book in Address Book.

Chapter 6

Getting Down to the Fun Stuff

● ●

In This Chapter

▶ Setting up e-mail accounts

▶ Browsing with Safari

▶ Touring the iTunes jukebox

▶ Getting pictures into your Mac

▶ Touching up photos

▶ Sharing your pictures

● ●

*I*n this chapter, you find out how to have fun with your Mac. You set up an e-mail account with Mac's Mail program and use the built-in Safari Web browser to find information and music on the Web. You also discover how Apple's convenient iTunes online store can help you find, download, and manage your music, and you see how the Mac's iPhoto software enables you to easily transfer your digital photos to your Mac and then touch them up like a professional!

Setting Up an E-Mail Account

Sending and reading e-mail through the Mac's Mail program is a breeze, once you set it up. And Mail setup has become simpler in Snow Leopard. I list several steps in this section, but if you're setting up an account with a mainstream provider, such as AOL, Comcast, Gmail, Verizon, or Yahoo!, you don't need to go beyond the second step:

1. **Open Mail by clicking the Mail icon (it looks like a stamp) on the dock or by double-clicking Mail in the Applications folder.**

   First-timers are greeted with a Welcome to Mail window, where you can set up an account using information from the .Mac pane of System Preferences (you must have a .Mac account).

2. **If you want to set up an e-mail account automatically:**

   • If you have a mainstream e-mail account (such as AOL, Comcast, Gmail, Verizon, or Yahoo!), enter your current e-mail address and password, and Apple will do the configuring on your behalf.

   • Otherwise, make sure Automatically Set Up Account is selected and click Create.

   If you run into snags, click the circle with the question mark at the bottom of the window or proceed to the next step.

3. **If you don't want to set up an e-mail account automatically, fill in your full name (this is what will be displayed in your outgoing messages), e-mail address, and password. Make sure Automatically Set Up Account is *not* selected. Click Continue.**

4. **Fill in the General Information required in the next screen.**

You must fill in an Account Type (from a drop-down menu), Description, Full Name, User Name, Password, and Incoming Mail Server. That last one is where your messages are retrieved; you'll enter something along the lines of **pop.** *yourprovider*.com.

5. **Add information about your outgoing server, which goes by the name of SMTP.**

Setting up additional mail accounts involves repeating these steps. Begin by choosing File⇨Add Account in Mail.

If the IMAPs and SMTPs and the rest are not exactly at your fingertips (and why should they be?), call your ISP or poke around the company's Web site for assistance. But again, you need not worry about such matters with most mainstream e-mail accounts.

Going on a Safari

Has the Internet somehow passed you by? Don't fret if you haven't boarded the cybershuttle just yet. Getting up to speed on the Internet isn't as daunting as you might think. You can enjoy a perfectly rewarding online experience through your Mac without ever deciphering the Net's most puzzling terms, everything from *domain names* to *file transfer protocols.* And you certainly don't have to stay up late cramming for any final exams.

Just browsing

To browse or surf the Web, you need a piece of software called, um, a *Web browser.* Because you had the good sense to purchase a Mac, you are blessed with one of the best browsers in the business. It's aptly named *Safari* because much of what you do in cyberspace is an expedition into the wild. See Figure 6-1.

Forward

Open in Dashboard

AutoFill form

Change font size

Report a bug to Apple

Web address field

Bookmarks bar

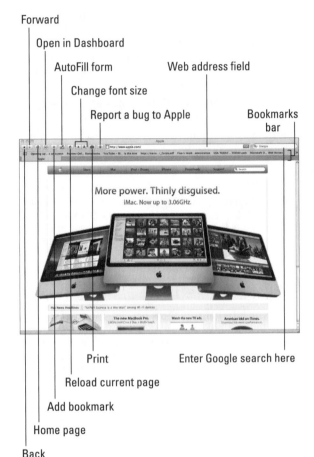

More power. Thinly disguised.
iMac. Now up to 3.06GHz.

Print

Enter Google search here

Reload current page

Add bookmark

Home page

Back

Figure 6-1: The Safari Web browser.

You enter the Web address, or URL, into an *address field* at the top of the browser window (labeled in Figure 6-1). As a Web page loads, a blue bar fills the address field to let you know the page is coming.

Web surfing would be awfully tedious if you had to type an address each time you wanted to go from one site to another. Fortunately, the bright minds who invented Safari and other browsers agree.

On the Safari *toolbar* you'll typically see a series of buttons or icons to the left of the address box where you entered the URL. The buttons you see and the order in which they appear vary, depending on how you customize the browser (refer to Figure 6-1 for a look at some of these buttons). To make the toolbar disappear entirely, choose View⇨Hide Toolbar. To make it reappear, choose View⇨Show Toolbar.

The left- and right-facing arrow buttons are the back and forward buttons, respectively. Click the left arrow to go to the last page you were looking at before the page that is currently displayed. Click the right arrow to advance to a page you've already looked at.

 Click the toolbar icon that looks like a house, and you go to your starting base, or *home page*. That's the site that greets you each time you fire up the browser for the first time. To change Safari's home page, choose Preferences from the Safari menu, click the General tab, and then type the Web address of your page of choice in the field labeled Home page.

You'll notice that some text on various Web pages is underlined in blue (or some other color). That means it's a *link*. Clicking a link takes you to another page without having to type any other instructions.

Tabbed browsing

Say you want to peek at several Web pages in a single browser window instead of having to open separate windows for each "open" page. Welcome to the high art of *tabbed browsing*. Visit Preferences in the Safari menu and then click Tabs. The window shown in

Figure 6-2 appears. Place check marks next to each of the settings you want.

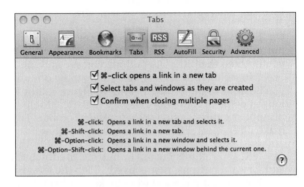

Figure 6-2: Keeping tabs. The tabbed browsing window.

Now each time you ⌘-click, you open a link in a new tab instead of a window. To toggle from one open Web page to another, just click its tab. The tabs appear just under the bookmarks bar.

To open a new tabbed window, choose File⇨New Tab or press ⌘+T.

 To rearrange the way that tabs appear, just drag them in any order.

Private browsing

Hey, maybe you have something to hide. Perhaps you're surfing in an Internet cafe. Or just possibly you're being paranoid. Whatever. Turn on a hush-hush Safari feature called *private browsing* by choosing that option on the Safari menu. Now Safari won't add the Web pages you've visited to the History menu (though you can still use the back and forward buttons to return to sites you've been to). When private browsing is turned on, AutoFill (discussed later) is turned off, searches are not added to the pop-up menu in the Google search box, and Web cookie preferences are also deep-sixed.

SnapBack

Sometimes you get carried away surfing, either while searching Google or just browsing the Web. In other words, you move from page to page to page to page. Before you know it you're in Never Never Web land. You can certainly keep clicking the back button until you return to your starting point. But by clicking the orange SnapBack icon that appears in the right side of the address field and the Google search box, you can return to square one without those excess clicks.

 To turn your current page to a SnapBack anchor point, choose History⇨Mark Page for SnapBack or press Option+⌘+K.

Using bookmarks

Odds are you'll rapidly get hooked on a bevy of juicy Web pages that become so irresistible you'll keep coming back for more. We won't ask, so you need not tell. Of course it's downright silly to have to remember and type the destination's Web address each time you return. Create a *bookmark* instead. The easiest way to add a bookmark is to click the + button in the toolbar. A dialog box appears (see Figure 6-3), asking you to type a name for the bookmark you have in mind and to choose a place to keep it for handy reference later. Clicking the Show All Bookmarks icon lets you manage all your bookmarks.

Figure 6-3: Where to book your bookmarks.

You can group bookmarks in menu folders called Collections. If you decide to bookmark the Internet Movie Database home page, for example, you might decide to place it in a Collections folder called Entertainment. Whenever you want to pay a return visit to the site, you open the Entertainment folder and click the bookmark.

Despite your best organizational skills, your list of bookmarks and Collections may become so, well, overbooked, that it becomes far less functional. I practically guarantee that you will tire of at least some of the sites now cluttering up your bookmarks closet. To delete a bookmark, highlight its name, click the Edit menu at the top of the screen, and then choose Cut. If you change your mind, choose Edit⇨Undo Delete Bookmark. If all that seems like too much work, highlight an unwanted bookmark and press the Delete button on your keyboard.

 You'll want to return to some sites so often they deserve VIP status. Reserve a spot for them in Safari's Bookmarks marquee, otherwise known as the *bookmarks bar,* situated below the browser's toolbar. Choose Bookmarks Bar when the dialog box pops up, asking where to place the bookmark you've just created.

Benefiting from History

Say you failed to bookmark a site and now, days later, you want to return. Only you can't remember what the darn place was called or the convoluted path that brought you there. Become a history major. Safari logs every Web page you open and keeps the record for about a week. So you can consult the History menu to view a list of all the sites you visited on a particular day during the week. Choose History⇨ Show All History or click History under the Bookmarks Collections to view a more complete historical record. You can even search for a site you visited by typing a keyword in the Bookmarks search field.

If you're wigged out by this Internet trail, you can always click Clear History to wipe the slate clean. Or choose the General tab under Safari Preferences and indicate whether you want to remove all traces of History after one day, one week, two weeks, one month, or one year — or to handle the job manually.

The tools of the trade for your Safari

Safari is capable of other neat tricks. I describe some of them in this section.

Pop-up blocker

Tolerating Web advertising is the price we pay for all the Web resources at our disposal. The problem is that some ads induce agita. The most offensive are *pop-ups,* those hiccupping nightmarish little windows that make you think you woke up in the middle of the Las Vegas strip. Pop-ups have the audacity to get between you and the Web page you are attempting to read. Turning on the pop-up blocker can shield you from such pollutants. Click Block Pop-Up Windows under the Safari menu. If a check mark appears, you have successfully completed your mission. Once in a great while, a pop-up is worth viewing; to turn off the pop-up blocker, simply repeat this exercise.

Google search bar

You can conduct a Google search by visiting www.
google.com. But Safari saves you the time and trouble. You can enter search terms directly in a box right on the toolbar.

Find

Now suppose you want to find all mentions of a particular term or phrase in the Web page you're viewing. Choose Edit⇨Find. Type the word you want to find, and Safari highlights all occurrences of the text. Apple's not leaving anything to chance; the rest of the page is dimmed so you can more easily make out those highlighted words. The number of matches is also displayed, as are arrows that let you go to the next or previous occurrence of the word.

Filling out forms

Safari can remember your name, address, passwords, and other information. So when you start typing a few characters in a Web form or other field, the browser can finish entering the text for you, provided it finds a match in its database. From the Safari menu, choose Preferences⇨AutoFill, and select the items you want Safari to use (such as info from your Address Book card). If several choices match the first several letters

you type, a menu appears. Press the arrow keys to
select the item you have in mind and then press Enter.

Web clipping

Dashboard widgets are handy little apps for looking
up phone numbers or getting sports scores. Safari
lets you create your own widgets, by clipping out a
section of a favorite Web page. The beauty is that you
are giving birth to a live widget that gets refreshed
whenever the underlying Web page is updated.
(You'll need Snow Leopard to take advantage of
this trick.)

In Safari, navigate to the Web page you want to trans-
form into a Dashboard widget, then click the Open in
Dashboard button (labeled in Figure 6-1).

The screen dims, except for a white rectangle that
appears and automatically wraps around various por-
tions on the page that seem like a natural section you
may want to clip. You can reposition this window so
that another section is highlighted. And if Apple still
doesn't highlight the portion you have in mind, click
inside the window to bring up handles so you can
drag until the window is expanded on the complete
section you want to snip out for your widget.

When you're satisfied, click Add. The Dashboard
appears with your newly created widget.

Report a bug to Apple

Hey, even Apple screws up sometimes. If you run into
trouble while browsing in Safari, click the Report a
Bug to Apple toolbar button (labeled in Figure 6-1). In
the box that appears, describe your issue and problem type (crash, can't log in, can't load page, and so
on). You can even send a screen shot of the page that
is giving you problems.

iTunes: The Great Mac Jukebox

As part of the iLife suite, iTunes is one of those melodious programs that musical enthusiasts (and everyone else) get just for owning a Mac.

Here's a rundown on what iTunes permits you to do:

- Listen to CDs
- *Rip,* or encode, the songs on a CD into music files that are compressed and stored in your digital library
- Add music to the library from the Internet
- Create, or *burn,* your own CDs or DVDs (with the proper CD or DVD burner, such as Apple's own Super Drive, which is included in some Macs)
- Listen to Internet radio by clicking the Radio icon in the source list to display a list of *streams* by category, such as Alt/Modern Rock and Blues
- Watch videos
- Organize your music by name, artist, time, album, genre, rating, and play count
- Segregate your music into customized playlists
- Stream or share the music in your library across a network — within certain limitations
- Create ringtones for your iPhone
- Transfer music onto an iPod or iPhone

To open iTunes, click the iTunes icon on the dock. This icon looks like a musical note resting on top of a CD.

Figure 6-4 shows you many of the iTunes controls, a few of which are described in the following list. (What you see may vary depending on the selections you make in the iTunes view options.)

Enter iTunes Store

Internet Radio

Source List

Back/previous track

Play/pause

Forward/next track

Volume

Now playing

Track status

Columns heads to sort

List view

Album view

Cover Flow view

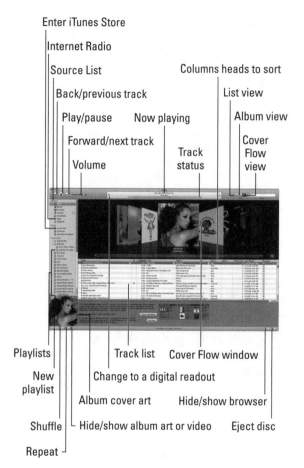

Playlists

New playlist

Shuffle

Repeat

Album cover art

Change to a digital readout

Hide/show album art or video

Track list

Cover Flow window

Hide/show browser

Eject disc

Figure 6-4: Ode to iTunes software.

✔ **Back/Forward:** The double arrows pointing to the left and right are your back and forward buttons, respectively. Place the cursor above these buttons and hold down the mouse to rewind or fast-forward through a song. If you instead single-click these arrows, you'll advance or retreat to the next or previous track.

✔ **Play/Pause:** Click the single arrow pointing to the right to play a song. When a song is playing, the button changes to two vertical bars. Click again to pause the music. Alternatively, press the spacebar to play or pause.

✔ **Volume:** Dragging this slider increases or decreases the volume.

✔ **List, Album, Cover Flow views:** To find music to listen to, you can rummage through album covers just as you once did with physical LPs. But if you prefer, you can view the contents of your iTunes stash using List view or Album view instead.

✔ **Shuffle:** When the symbol in this little button is highlighted (it turns blue), tracks play in random order. Be prepared for anything. There's no telling when Eminem will follow The Wiggles.

✔ **Repeat:** Click once to repeat all the songs in the library or playlist you're currently listening to. Click twice so that the number 1 appears on the button. Only the current track will repeat.

Ripping audio CDs

So how exactly does music make its way into iTunes? And what exactly happens to the songs after you have 'em? I thought you'd never ask.

A remarkable thing happens moments after you insert the vast majority of music CDs into your Mac. Typically, iTunes opens, and the contents of the disc — song titles, artist name, length, album name, and genre — are automatically recognized and copied into iTunes. Now here's another remarkable feat: Next time, you won't have to keep inserting said CD into the computer to hear its music. That's because you can rip, or copy, the contents onto the Mac's hard drive, and then stash the disc somewhere else.

A pop-up asks if you'd like to copy the album. Agree, and all songs with a checkmark next to their name will be copied; be sure to click to deselect any songs you have no interest in before proceeding. In some instances, you'll copy a CD by clicking the Import CD button at the bottom-right corner of the window instead.

Incidentally, you can listen to the CD (or do other work) while ripping a disc. After iTunes has completed its mission, remove the CD by clicking Eject (the rightmost icon at the bottom of the screen). Copied songs are stored in the iTunes library.

If you weren't connected to the Internet and couldn't grab song names when copying a disc, you don't need to reinsert the CD into the computer the next time you are on the Internet. Select the songs and choose Advanced⇨Get CD Track Names.

Finding music (and more) online

iTunes serves as a gateway to a delightful emporium for music lovers. The iTunes Store is where hunting for songs is a pleasure for all but the most tone-deaf users. Don't believe me? How else to explain more than 5 billion downloads since Apple opened the place? To enter the store, click iTunes Store in the source list.

Sadly, you won't find every song on your wish list because some performers or the music labels that control the artists' catalogues foolhardily remain digital holdouts and have yet to put their records up for sale in cyberspace.

 Shopping online for music affords you many privileges. Most notably, you have the opportunity to cherry-pick favorite tracks from an album, without having to buy the entire compilation. Note, however, that some record labels require that some tracks be purchased only as part of a full-blown album.

What's more, you can sample all the tracks for 30 seconds, without any obligation to buy. Most of the songs that you do choose to buy cost 99¢ a pop.

When you're ready to buy

Are you ready to spend some money? First, you have to set up an account with Apple (assuming you haven't already done so) or use an existing AOL account:

1. **In the Source List, click iTunes Store.**

2. **In the sign-in window, click Create New Account.**

3. **Fill in the requested credit card and other info.**

4. **The rest is easy. Find a song you want to buy and click Buy Song.**

   To make sure you really mean it, Apple serves up a warning.

5. **Click Buy to complete the transaction.**

   In a matter of seconds (usually) the song is downloaded to the aptly named Purchased playlist. But the purchased track typically has restrictions.

Getting Pictures in the Computer

In the past, it was a challenge to get digital images into your computer. iPhoto drastically simplifies the process. Take a gaze at Figures 6-5 and 6-6 to familiarize yourself with some of the program's main elements. You're peeking at the Events view in the first figure and the Photos view in the second.

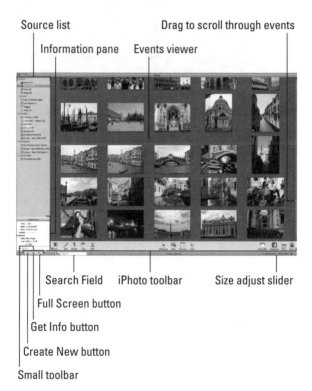

Source list — Drag to scroll through events

Information pane — Events viewer

Search Field — iPhoto toolbar — Size adjust slider

Full Screen button

Get Info button

Create New button

Small toolbar

Figure 6-5: Zooming in on iPhoto Events.

Viewer   Scroll guide

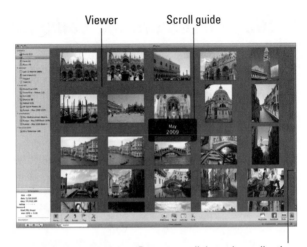

Drag to scroll through a collection

Figure 6-6: The Photos view of iPhoto.

Connecting a digital camera

In most cases, you run a direct connection from the digital camera to the Mac by connecting the USB cable supplied with the camera. Turn the camera off and then plug one end of the cable into the camera and the other end into the Mac. Turn the camera back on.

iPhoto opens, assuming you clicked Yes when the program asked whether you want to use iPhoto to download photos when a camera is connected. (This question pops up the first time you launch the program.) The way iPhoto takes charge, you won't even have to install the software that came with your camera. Given how cumbersome some of these programs can be, that, my friends, is a blessing.

If you run into a problem, you can try the following:

- ✔ Check to make sure your camera is turned on and you have a fresh set of batteries.

- ✔ Because every camera is different, consult the instructions that came with your model to make sure it's in the proper setting for importing pictures (usually Play mode).

Importing images from the camera

When you connect a camera and iPhoto comes to life, the camera name appears under Devices in the source list to the left of the screen, and your pictures show up in the main viewing area, as you can see in Figure 6-7.

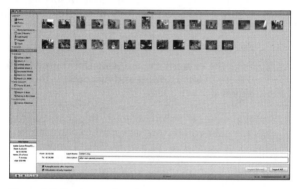

Figure 6-7: Getting ready to import your pictures.

To transfer images, follow these steps:

1. **Type an event name (for example, Father's Day) and a description (such as, after dad opened presents) in the appropriate fields.**

2. **If the pictures span a few days, select the Autosplit Events After Importing option to split the collection into several different events.**

3. **If you already imported some of the pictures in the camera, select Hide Photos Already Imported so you won't see them in the window.**

4. **To import only select pictures from this batch, press the ⌘ key and click the pictures you want to include. Click Import Selected.**

5. **Click Import All to transfer the pictures to iPhoto's digital shoebox.**

   The process may take several minutes depending on a variety of factors, including the number of images being imported. A counter indicates how many pictures remain to be copied.

6. **When the program has finished importing, a window gives you the option to delete the originals on the camera or keep them.**

   Entirely your call, my friend.

7. **Drag the camera's name from the source list to iPhoto trash. Turn off and disconnect the camera.**

Seeing double? If iPhoto detects a duplicate photo it asks whether you're sure you want to copy it over again. Click Import to proceed or Don't Import to skip this particular image. To avoid getting this question for each duplicate image, select Apply to All Duplicates.

iPhoto will also copy over movie clips from your digital camera, provided they're compatible with QuickTime. These videos are automatically transferred in the same way as still images.

Importing images from other sources

Not all the pictures in your iPhoto library arrive by
direct transfer from your digital camera. Some reach
the Mac by the Web, e-mail, CDs or DVDs, flash
drives, or memory card readers. Other pictures may
already reside somewhere else on your hard drive.

To get these pictures into iPhoto, drag them into the
iPhoto viewing area or onto the iPhoto dock icon. You
can drag individual pictures or an entire folder or
disk. Or choose File⇨Import to Library and browse
for the files you want to bring over. Then click Import.

iPhoto is compatible with JPEG and TIFF, the
most common image file formats, as well as PNG
and a photo enthusiast format (available on
some digital cameras) known as RAW.

Touching Up Your Photos

Here's a dirty little secret. The drop-dead gorgeous
models gracing the covers of magazines don't really
look like that. (Well maybe some do, but work with
me here.) The unsung heroes are the touch-up artists,
who remove a flaw from a picture here, a blemish
there. We should all be so lucky to be able to put our
own mugs in the best light. And lucky we are for
having iPhoto.

Now iPhoto is by no means a photo-editing superstar
along the lines of Adobe's Photoshop or Apple's own
Aperture. But for the mainstream snapshooter, iPhoto
comes with several handy editing tools for removing
red eye and applying special effects.

I'll get around to these in a moment. But first let's examine a majestic way to display your images in iPhoto that
can help you take advantage of every last pixel.

The full-screen treatment

iPhoto's full-screen viewing option lets you exploit today's large and beautiful computer displays. What's more, Apple lets you edit in this mode.

To enter the full-screen edit mode, select a photo from the main viewing area and click the Full-Screen button (labeled in Figure 6-5). When you roll your mouse at the *top* of the screen, a strip of thumbnails called the *photo browser* (see Figure 6-8) slides in and out of view. Roll your mouse to the bottom of the screen to slide the various editing tools into view.

Photo browser

Editing tools

Figure 6-8: Full-screen editing majesty.

You can compare between two and eight photos in the full-screen view by holding ⌘ while clicking thumbnails in the photo browser. If you click the Compare button instead, the photo you choose is compared with the one to its immediate right.

If you prefer the full-screen view all the time, go to iPhoto Preferences and click the General tab. Under the Edit Photo drop-down list, select Using Full Screen. To exit the full-screen mode, press the Escape key.

If you want to edit photos in the conventional view instead, double-click a thumbnail in the viewing area, and the same editing tools you see in full-screen view appear below the selected image. If they don't appear, highlight a picture and click Edit in the menu bar. Let's have a look at some of those editing buttons now.

Rotating an image

Sometimes a picture that turns up in the photo library is oriented incorrectly. To fix the orientation in iPhoto, select the image and click Rotate on the editing toolbar, at the bottom of the screen. The image rotates counterclockwise by 90 degrees. Keep clicking until the picture is oriented properly. Press the Option key while clicking to make the picture flip the other way.

Cropping an image

Cropping means snipping away at the periphery of an image. This technique allows you to get up close and personal to the subject at hand while removing traces of that yo-yo in the background who is sticking out his tongue.

To crop an image:

1. **Click Crop on the editing toolbar.**

2. **Choose the cropping area.**

   To limit the crop area to a specific dimension, select the Constrain check box (if it's not already selected) and make a selection.

3. **Drag the crop area into the proper position.**

4. **Click Apply and then Done to save your changes.**

If you're unhappy with a newly cropped picture, choose Edit⇨Undo. And at any time, you can choose Photos⇨Revert to Original and pretend that nothing happened.

If you want to crop an image *and* keep the original, choose Photos⇨Duplicate. Give the cloned picture a name and do your cropping on it.

Repairing blemishes

What do you do when that otherwise immaculate portrait is ruined by a small stain on your sweater? Click Retouch on the editing toolbar to turn on iPhoto's high-tech spot remover. Drag the slider to select a brush size. Then hold down the mouse button as you brush over that spot, freckle, blotch, or pimple. iPhoto paints over these spots using surrounding colors. Use short strokes to avoid smearing an image and making the picture appear ghoulish. Alternatively, click over a small spot you want to remove. Click Retouch again when you're finished. Retouching larger images is easier than smaller ones, making full-screen mode all the more valuable when editing thusly.

Straightening

Does the photo you took appear crooked? Or maybe you just can't come to terms with the fact that the leaning tower of Pisa is actually *leaning.* Clicking Straighten brings up a slider that lets you rotate a picture 10 degrees or less in either direction.

Enhancing and adjusting

The quick-fix Enhance tool automatically brightens a faded or too-dark image or adjusts one that's too bright by correcting the image's color saturation and tint. Click the Enhance button once, and iPhoto does the rest. In reality, the picture isn't always enhanced, but as usual you have a variety of undo options.

While iPhoto does all the work for you inside Enhance, Adjust puts the onus on *you*. Clicking Adjust brings up a palette. Manually drag the sliders to adjust the exposure, contrast, highlights and shadows, color saturation, and other elements. If you get totally lost after messing with these settings, click Reset to start from scratch.

Reducing red-eye

Flash photography often results in *red-eye,* where it looks like your subject is auditioning for the lead role in *Rosemary's Baby: All Grown Up.* To get rid of it, click the Red-Eye button and place the crosshairs pointer in the center of each red eye. Or use the size slider to zoom in on each reddened pupil and click. Click the Red-Eye button again to complete the exorcism.

Admiring and Sharing Pictures

Until now, I've been speaking of importing and doctoring images. Enough of that. It's time to sit back and admire your handiwork and show off your skills to everyone else.

Creating slideshows

If you're of a certain generation, you may remember having to sit still while your parents pulled out the Kodak Carousel Slide Projector. "There we are in front of the Grand Canyon. There we are in front of the Grand Canyon — *from a slightly different angle.*"

The twenty-first-century slideshow, in care of a Mac, brings a lot more pizzazz. Your pictures are backed with a soundtrack from your iTunes library. And you can slowly zoom in and out of photos employing the Ken Burns Effect, named after the documentary filmmaker.

To create a slideshow, follow these steps:

1. **Choose the album or groups of photos you want in your show.**

2. **Click the Add (+) button on the toolbar and then click the Slideshow tab.**

3. **Choose a name (if it's not already filled in with an album name) for the slideshow and make sure the Use Selected Items in New Slideshow option is selected.**

4. **Click Create and drag pictures in the order you want them to play in the photo browser at the top of the viewing area.**

   The name of your slideshow is now in the source list under a Slideshows heading.

5. **Click Music to choose a soundtrack from iTunes or sample music included with iPhoto.**

6. **Click Settings, make your selections, and then click OK.**

7. **If you want to tweak settings for individual slides, click Adjust.**

8. **To preview visual changes to slides in a smaller window without sound, click Preview.**

9. **Click Play to get on with the show.**

 You can rotate and rate pictures in a slideshow on-the-fly or pause the show by moving your cursor onto the screen.

You can burn your slideshow to a DVD, share it online, or export it to a QuickTime movie.

E-mailing pictures

To send pictures using e-mail, highlight an image (or hold down the ⌘ key to send a bunch of photos) in your library or an album and click the Mail button on the iPhoto toolbar. A dialog box asks you to choose a size for the photo (small, medium, large, or actual size).

Before clicking Compose Message, decide whether you want to include the titles, descriptions, and location information with your photo by selecting those options (or not).

Click Compose. Snow Leopard's Mail program opens with the picture already attached (assuming Mail is your default e-mail application). Fill in the recipient's address, type a subject line, and add any additional prose before sending the picture on its merry way.

 Visit iPhoto Preferences if you want to send e-mail through another mail program such as AOL, Eudora, or Microsoft Entourage.

You can also e-mail pictures as attachments through such Web-based e-mail programs as Gmail, Hotmail, and Yahoo! Mail.

Booking them

There aren't many guarantees in life. But one of them is that bound coffee-table photo books of the family make splendid presents. Apple makes it a breeze to design these professionally printed books. And when the grandparents see what *you* produced, don't be shocked if they ask how come you're not working in the publishing business.

From iPhoto, you choose the size and design of these books and the batch of photos to be included. Images are sent over the Internet to a printing plant, which binds and ships the book (within days) on your behalf to its final destination. Apple's large hardcover photo books start around $30 (for 20 pages/10 sheets). Medium and large softcover versions start at $10 to $20, respectively. Small-sized 2.6-by-3.5-inch books (sold three books at a time) fetch $12. *Note:* You need to have an AppleID and a valid credit card to purchase a photo book.

Here's how to go about designing a photo book:

1. **Choose the albums or photos.**

2. **Click the Add (+) button at the bottom left and select the Book tab.**

   The Book Type dialog box appears.

3. **Enter a name, and select the size of the book, whether you want hardcover or softcover, and the design.**

   Among your choices are Picture Book, Formal, Travel, and Family Album. Some themes let you type text with your pictures. For detailed descriptions, click the Options + Pricing button.

4. **Click a theme.**

   You are now in *book view.* The current page of your book appears in the main iPhoto viewer, below a thumbnail strip of pictures you can manually drag onto photo placeholders in the page layouts.

5. **If you want to fatten your book, click Add Pages on the editing toolbar.**

6. **To determine the layout of pictures on a page and whether to add text, click Layout.**

   If you want iPhoto to arrange your book for you (it's not nearly as much fun), choose Autoflow.

7. **When you're satisfied, click Buy Book and enter your AppleID and credit card and shipping information.**

You can also turn the contents of your book into a slideshow. Choose the book (found under Projects in the source list) and click the Play button. You can change transitions, choose background music, and tweak other settings, as described with regular slideshows earlier.

Chapter 7

Handling Trouble

● ●

In This Chapter

▶ Fixing a cranky or frozen computer

▶ Finishing off Startup problems

▶ Repairing common problems

● ●

I'm reluctant to morph into Mr. Doom-and-gloom all of a sudden, but after reading about all the wonderful things Macs can do, it is my unpleasant duty to point out that bad @#$& happens. Even on a Mac.

Fortunately, most issues are minor. A stubborn mouse. Tired hardware. Disobedient software. Under the most dire circumstances, your computer or a key component within is on its last legs. After all, a Mac, like any computer, is a machine. Still, rarely is a problem beyond fixing. So stay calm, scan through this chapter, and with luck you'll come across a trouble-shooting tip to solve your issue.

A Cranky Computer

Your Mac was once a world-class sprinter but now can barely jog. Here are four possible explanations, and a fix to go with each one.

- ✔ **Your Mac needs more memory.** The programs you're running may demand more RAM than you have on hand. I always recommend getting as much memory as your computer (and wallet) permit. Adding RAM to the recent class of Mac machines isn't difficult (check your computer's documentation for specifics), though it does involve cracking open the case and making sure you're buying the right type of memory.

- ✔ **Your Mac is running out of hard drive space.** This is an easy one: Remove programs or files you no longer use. There must be something you can live without. But if every last bit is indispensable, purchase an additional drive.

- ✔ **Your Mac's processor, or CPU, is overtaxed.** If you suspect this might be the case, open the Activity Monitor, by choosing Applications⇨ Utilities. Activity Monitor reveals a lot about the programs and processes currently running on your machine. Click the CPU header to display the applications exacting the heaviest workload on your CPU (*central processing unit*). The most demanding are on top. Quit those you don't need at the moment.

- ✔ **The Mac may be trying to save energy.** On a laptop, the Mac may be slowing the processor purposely. Choose ⚫⇨System Preferences and click Energy Saver. Use the Optimization pop-up menu near the top to switch from Better Energy Savings to Better Performance.

A Frozen Computer or Program

It isn't often that a frozen program will crash the entire system, but it does happen. A beach ball that spins — and spins, and spins some more — is a sign that a cranky Mac has turned into a frozen Mac or that at least one of the programs on the machine is throwing a high-tech temper tantrum. (In some cases, you may see a spinning gear cursor instead.) Your first instinct is to stick a pin inside this virtual *spinning beach ball of death*, if only you knew how. If you're a model of patience, you can attempt to wait the problem out and hope the spinning eventually stops. If it doesn't, consider the options described in this section.

Force Quit

Force Quit is the Mac's common way of telling an iced application, "I'm as mad as hell and I'm not going to take it anymore." (If you're too young, that's a reference to the 1976 movie *Network,* as in television network.)

Choose ⌘⇨Force Quit or press ⌘+Option+Esc. Click the name of the deviant application ("not responding" probably appears next to its name). Under Force Quit you typically won't have to reboot your computer.

Because you will lose any unsaved changes, Apple throws up a little admonition before allowing you to Force Quit. Alas, you may have no choice.

Ctrl-clicking a dock icon brings up a pop-up menu whose bottom item is Quit. If you hold down the Option key, Quit becomes Force Quit.

When a program quits on you

When programs suddenly drop, you might see dialog boxes with the word *quit unexpectedly.* Sometimes the box lets you click to Reopen the fussy program;

sometimes the option is to Try Again. OS X restores the application's default settings (thus setting aside newer preferences settings), in case something you did (imagine that?) caused the snafu.

Assuming everything went swell from there, you'll be given the option of keeping the new settings upon quitting the program. Your old preferences are saved in a file with a *.saved* extension, in case you ever want to go back. If that is the case, move the newer and current preferences file from its present location and remove the .saved extension from the older file.

If you feel like doing your itty-bitty part to help Apple make things right in the future, you can share a problem report with the company. Apple won't directly get in touch with you about the issue.

If the problem continues, it may be time to visit the library. No, not that kind of library. A Preferences folder lives inside your Library folder, which in turn resides in your Home folder. Whew! Got it? These preferences files have the *.plist* suffix and typically begin with *com.* followed by the names of the developer and program, as in *com.microsoft.Word.plist.* Try dragging a *.plist* file with the name of the troubled application out to the desktop. If the program runs smoothly, trash the corrupted preferences file.

Just to keep you on your toes, a separate Preferences folder resides inside a separate Library folder inside your Macintosh HD folder (which you can click on the left side of the Finder). You may have to repeat this drill there.

Forcing a restart

Force Quit will usually rescue you from a minor problem, but it's not effective all the time. If that's the situation you're in now, you'll likely have to reboot. The

assumption here is that your frozen computer won't
permit you to start over in a conventional way by
choosing ⬆⇨Restart.

Instead, try holding down the power button for several seconds or press Ctrl+⌘ and then the power
button. If all else fails, pull the plug (or remove the
battery from a laptop), though only as a last resort.

Safe boot

To start in Safe mode, press the power button to turn
on your computer, and press and hold the Shift key
the instant you hear the familiar welcome chime.
Release Shift when the Apple logo appears. You'll
know you've done it correctly because the words *Safe
Boot* appear in the login window.

Because of its under-the-hood machinations, it
will take considerably longer to boot in Safe
mode. This is perfectly normal. So is the fact
that you can't use AirPort, a USB modem, or
your DVD player, you can't capture footage in
iMovie, and you can't use certain other applications or features.

If the Safe boot resolved your issue, restart the Mac
normally next time, without pressing Shift. If not, it
might be time to check your warranty or call in an
expert.

Startup Problems

I just discussed a few ways to handle a cranky Mac.
But what if you can't even start the Mac? This is a
very unusual circumstance. You probably have no
power because the plug came loose (blame it on the
dog), the switch on the power strip is off, your

battery ran out of juice, or there's a blackout in your neighborhood. Did you even notice that the lights went out?

On some laptops, you can tell if a battery needs recharging by pressing a small button on the battery. Lights on the battery let you know how much strength the battery has.

Here's another thing to try: Press power and hold down the ⌘, Option, P, and R keys and wait until you hear the startup chime a second time.

If you've added memory, installed an AirPort Card, or installed another component and the machine fails to start, make sure the installation is correct and try again. If your computer still can't be revived, try removing the memory or card you just installed and then give it another shot.

After that, if you still can't restart, you may have to seek warranty service, as discussed later in this chapter.

Common Fixes to Other Problems

Sometimes all your Mac needs is a little first aid rather than major surgery. In this section, I consider some minor snags.

A jumpy mouse

Real mice live for dust and grime. And so for a long time did computer rodents. But the optical-style mice included with the most recent Macs don't get stuck like their ancestors because this kind of critter doesn't use the little dust-collecting rolling ball on its underbelly.

Be aware that optical mice don't like glass or reflective surfaces, so if you find your mouse on one, place a mouse pad or piece of paper underneath.

If your mouse doesn't respond at all, unplug it from the USB port and then plug it in again, just to make sure the connection is snug. If you have a wireless mouse, make sure it is turned on and the batteries are fresh.

A stuck CD

It's cool the way most Macs practically suck up a CD. Here's what's not cool: when the drive, particularly the slot-loading kind, won't spit out the disc.

Take a stab at one of these fixes:

- ✔ Quit the program using the disc and then press Eject on the keyboard.

- ✔ Open a Finder window, and click the little eject icon in the sidebar. Or try dragging the disc icon from the Mac desktop to the trash.

- ✔ Log out of your user account (under the menu) and then press Eject on the keyboard.

- ✔ Restart the computer while holding down the mouse button.

My Mac can no longer tell time

If your computer can no longer keep track of the time and date, its internal backup battery may have bit the dust. On some models, you can't replace this battery yourself; you'll have to contact the Apple store or an authorized service provider.

The wrong program answers the call of duty

The Mac makes certain assumptions about which application ought to open a particular file when summoned. For example, Preview is Snow Leopard's document viewer of choice and routinely handles JPEG graphics and PDF documents, and *.doc* files are the province of Microsoft Word. But say you want the Adobe programs Photoshop and Reader to be responsible for JPEGs and PDFs, and Mac's own word processor, TextEdit, to take care of DOC duties?

Here's what to do:

1. **Highlight the icon of the file you want opened by a different application and press ⌘+I.**

2. **In the Get Info panel that appears, click the right-facing triangle next to Open With and choose the application to handle the document from here on out.**

   In this example, I've taken a *.doc* file that would otherwise open in Word and put TextEdit in charge. Incidentally, if you want to open the file from a different parent than Apple suggests, choose Other from the pop-up menu.

   Alternatively, access the Open With command by highlighting the file icon in question and choosing File➪Open With. You can also bring up the Get Info pane from the same menu. Still another way to get to Open With: Press Control while clicking the icon (or right-click if your mouse has two buttons).

3. **If you want the application to open each and every file of this type that you beckon in the future, click Change All.**

Kernel clink

Out of the blue, you are asked to restart your computer. In numerous languages, no less. Your machine has been hit with a *kernel panic*. The probable cause is corrupted or incompatible software. (One of these panics can also be induced by damaged hardware, although that is highly unlikely.)

The good news is that a system restart usually takes care of the problem with no further harm. If it doesn't, try removing any memory or hardware you've recently added. Of if you think some new software you installed may have been the culprit, head to the software publisher's Web site and see whether it's issued a downloadable fix or upgrade.

SOS for DNS

If you're surfing the Web and get a message about a DNS entry not being found, you typed the wrong Web address or URL, the site in question no longer exists (or never did), or the site is having temporary problems. DNS is computer jargon for *Domain Name System* or *Server*. Similar messages may be presented as a *404 not found on this server* error.

Curing the trash can blues

In the physical world, you may try and throw something out of your trash can but can't because the rubbish gets stuck to the bottom of the can. The virtual trash can on your Mac sometimes suffers a similar fate: A file refuses to budge when you click Empty Trash in the Finder menu.

Try junking the files by holding down the Option key when you choose Empty Trash.

A file might refuse to go quietly for several reasons. For starters, you can't delete an item that is open somewhere else on your computer, so make sure the item is indeed closed. Moreover, you may be trying to ditch a file to which you do not have sufficient permission. The other most likely explanation is that a locked file is in the trash. You can unlock it by choosing File⇨Get Info and making sure the Locked box is not selected.

After a program unexpectedly crashes, one or more Recovered Files folders may appear in your trash after a restart. Temporary files are often used and disposed of by your applications, but during a crash the files may not get disposed. If any of these files are valuable, drag them out of trash. More often than not, however, it is safe to discard them with the rest of the garbage.

Chapter 8

Ten Clever Dashboard Widgets

*T*hink of the Dashboard widgets of Chapter 6 fame as a reflection of our busy lives. We're all distracted, pressed for time, going every which way. We generally know what we want, and we want it now. In this fast-food society, snack software seems inevitable.

In this chapter, I present in alphabetical order a list of ten yummy widgets. With more than 4,800 widgets

available as of this writing on Apple's site, you can
easily come up with a menu of ten more widgets, and
ten more after that. And so on. To find them at Apple,
head to www.apple.com/downloads/dashboard.
You can also search cyberspace for other dashboard
widgets. Most widgets are free, though donations are
often requested.

Cocktail

Can you mix an, um, Apple Martini? Kamikaze? Or
Piper at the Gates of Dawn? The free Cocktail widget
from Seven lets you impress buddies with your mixol-
ogist skills. Just type the drink you have in mind.
Cocktail's database includes nearly 7,000 drink reci-
pes. Click "Feelin Thirsty?" for a random selection.
With its martini-glass icon, shown in Figure 8-1,
Cocktail has one of the better-looking widgets too.

Figure 8-1: I'll have a Cocktail with that widget.

Countdown Plus

Hmm. Steven Chaitoff's simple Countdown Plus
widget tells you how much time is remaining until a
specified date, such as the newborn's due date, your
next vacation, your anniversary, or the day you'll be
paroled.

Gas

I loath paying a small ransom at the pump. Gas from Jason Barry might help you save a few pennies per gallon. The widget delivers information from GasPriceWatch.com and has links to AAA gas data. You can sort results by Regular, Plus, Premium, or Diesel and set preferences to find stations within one to fifteen miles of a designated Zip code. What's more, click the address of the gas station of choice, and the widget fires up Google Maps on your browser. The Gas widget is free, but its producers hope you'll pass along some of your savings to them (via PayPal). You can display the widget with a pole or without.

Hurricane Tracker

If you live or expect to vacation in an area affected by hurricanes, Hurricane Tracker and Hurricane Tracker Companion from Travel Widgets are useful resources (see Figure 8-2 for a peek at both). The front of Hurricane Tracker includes text links to the National Hurricane Center advisories; satellite imagery is on the back. The Companion widget lets you choose how you want satellite images to appear (Visible, Infrared, Water Vapor).

Figure 8-2: Tracking storms.

iStat pro

Former New York City Mayor Ed Koch used to always
ask, "How am I doing?" This customizable system monitor widget from iSlayer.com lets you quickly get a
sense of how your Mac is doing. As Figure 8-3 shows,
you can check out CPU, memory and disk usage, gauge
temperature sensors, and more.

Figure 8-3: A quick way to monitor your Mac.

Movies

Want to know the flicks playing in the hood? Want to
read a synopsis and view trailers to help you decide
which to see? That's just what Movies (see Figure 8-4),
a simple film fan widget from Apple, lets you do. Apple
supplied the widget with Snow Leopard. It even lets
you purchase tickets (via Fandango). Now let's see,
Vicky Christina Barcelona or *The Dark Knight* . . .

Figure 8-4: A going-to-the-movies widget.

pearLyrics/Sing that iTune

Sad refrain. One of my favorite widgets, pearLyrics, is no longer available, apparently over legal disputes with some in the music industry. I mention it anyway because it still works on my machine and the idea behind it is so appealing to any music fan who has ever wanted to sing along but can't remember the words. Besides, you can still download a similar widget called Sing that iTune.

The two widgets display the lyrics of songs you're listening to in iTunes, at least a decent part of the time. And Sing that iTune, unlike pearLyrics, displays album cover art. It also lets you download artwork, save lyrics in iTunes, and search for Japanese or Chinese lyrics. Who knows, maybe pearLyrics will return someday. In the meanwhile, check out Sing that iTune.

Send SMS

SMS stands for Short Message Service, a popular global standard for dispatching text messages to cell phones. This widget from SMS Mac lets you send text messages to a mobile phone from your keyboard. You type your missive in the area provided on the front of the widget, and then click to flip it over to enter a recipient and a phone number.

Your first purchase totals $15 (you can pay through PayPal) and covers the $10 annual fee and first 50 SMS messages ($5). Not cheap.

Wikipedia

With the free collaborative Wikipedia encyclopedia, you can search on most any topic imaginable. Or try clicking the little ? button next to the search field to display an article randomly, on subjects ranging from the Danish parliamentary election of 1975 to nineteenth-century cowboy outlaw William "Curly Bill" Brocius (or Brocious — Wikipedia isn't sure). Indeed, anyone can contribute to a Wikipedia entry, so the information you uncover may be open to interpretation and possibly inaccurate. Click the Wikipedia button in the widget to jump to the full Wikipedia site.

Word of the Day

I'm feeling rather *sedulous*. After all, I'm diligent in my application or pursuit and steadily industrious. Besides, sedulous is my Word of the Day, delivered by a widget of the same name. Definitions (like the one provided in the sentence before this one) are supplied by Dictionary.com.

Those of you seeking to bolster your vocabulary are kindly encouraged to make a donation.

After you've read the Portable Edition, look for the original Dummies book on the topic. The handy Contents at a Glance below highlights the information you'll get when you purchase a copy of *Macs For Dummies*, 10th Edition — available wherever books are sold, or visit dummies.com.

Contents at a Glance